**FATAL
ERROR**

FATAL ERROR

confessions

of an

accidental

killer

thomas munch-petersen

✳ SHORT BOOKS

First published in 2003 by

Short Books

15 Highbury Terrace

London N5 1UP

10 9 8 7 6 5 4 3 2 1

A CIP catalogue record for this book
is available from the British Library.

ISBN 1-904095-45-3

Printed in Great Britain by

Bookmarque Ltd, Croydon, Surrey

Thomas Munch-Petersen is a senior lecturer in Scandinavian history at University College London. He has two sons and lives on the south coast.

For Jannie, my rock through all the storms, and for David, who proved in the darkest times the sort of man his father would have wished to be.

Contents

I   IN LIMBO

Chapter One
Pinxton (10 April 2000)

I still have flashbacks. They come like shadows thrown across the landscape by mixed sunshine and cloud. I see everything in slow motion, but at the same time I retain an overwhelming sensation of suddenness and confusion. The flashbacks are mostly a series of snapshots – the central barrier of the motorway and the traffic streaming south beyond it, the lorry on its side leaking diesel, the two wrecked cars lying crushed in the sunlight.

The accident happened just before one o'clock in the afternoon on Monday, 10 April 2000 near the Pinxton junction on the M1 motorway. Three people died and a fourth was seriously injured. And I am to blame for it.

I had left my home in south-west London about three hours earlier and was driving north, headed for Leeds. I had stopped for lunch around noon at a motorway refreshment centre, and set off again after about half an hour. I was travelling alone and, when I left, I drooped my jacket over the front passenger seat.

The accident came twenty minutes later. I was in the fast lane, doing seventy miles an hour. I had almost completed overtaking three or four cars in the middle lane and I recall thinking that I would soon be able to move back into the middle lane myself. I had developed a bitter taste in my mouth since lunch, and I decided to lift my jacket off the passenger seat and on to my lap so as to be able to get some mints out of the left side-pocket.

Taking my left hand off the steering wheel to reach for my jacket was a terrible misjudgement – and it had terrible consequences. I was not holding the steering wheel tightly enough with my right hand and as I started to lift up the jacket, I noticed that my car was drifting towards the middle lane. As I was later to learn, the period of my distraction from the road ahead was less than two seconds.

When I realised what was happening, I was very frightened that I might continue into the middle lane and collide with the last of the cars I had been overtaking. My reaction was to throw the jacket away from me, put my left hand back on the wheel and turn sharply right. This immediately produced a new crisis, because it put my car on collision course with the central barrier of the motorway. I was terrified that I would smash through the barrier into the southbound carriageway.

In my panic, I now turned sharply left – much too sharply left. I veered across the motorway. I desperately tried to straighten the car, but it was too late and I collided diagonally with the side of a lorry that was travelling in the inner lane. Those few seconds as the lorry loomed before me like a great ocean liner were moments of pure, cold fear.

The front left-hand side of my car seemed to crumple like cardboard in the collision, but I was unhurt and still thought I could control the car. I tried to pull away from the lorry, but found that I couldn't. It felt as if the lorry were chasing me. It seemed to be glued to the side of my car and to be carrying me along with it. I thought of a leaf borne on the crest of a great wave. By now, my windscreen was partially shattered and the bonnet of my car had flown up so I could not see what was happening around me or to me. I recall the sounds of several tremendous collisions and the sensation of my car spinning helplessly out of control.

And then, suddenly, the car had come to a stop and I was astonished to see that I was in the southbound carriageway facing towards the northbound carriageway at virtually a right angle. Everything now seemed very quiet after the noise and movement of the preceding moments. I guess that between reaching for my jacket and my car coming to a stop, no more than a minute or two had passed.

I first looked to the right and saw that all three lanes of southbound traffic had come to a halt only a few yards away from me. The cars stacked up, one behind the other, made me think of crows sitting on the branches of a tall, dead tree. I then looked to my left and saw that the lorry was lying on its side with its great wheels pointing at me and that diesel was leaking freely from it onto the road between us. There were thin billows of smoke drifting up from my engine.

The left side of my car had crumpled around me, but the interior was undamaged and I was unhurt except for a tiny splinter of glass from the windshield lodged in one finger. I was numbed and dazed, and for a time I just sat behind the wheel of my car. It cannot have been for longer than a few seconds, since I quickly realised that the leaking diesel might be a deadly threat both to the lorry driver and to me. I got out of my car and hurried round to look into the cab of the lorry to make sure the driver was not trapped. His windscreen was shattered and he was not there, but I saw a man in a dark anorak lying face down on the grass verge nearby. I noticed that there were two crashed cars further south on the motorway and that several southbound travellers had already stopped and were running towards the damaged vehicles.

The following hour is a jumble of confused impressions. I recall kneeling by the lorry driver, who was alive but unconscious, and running back to my car to get the first-aid kit in the glove compartment, while two or three people tried to help him. I passed most of the time sitting on the grass verge between the lorry and the first of the crashed cars. I remember speaking to a number of people. One was a man with a moustache and a Midlands accent. He was very gentle. At one point, he knelt beside me and stroked my hair to comfort me. But he also displayed a certain ghoulish curiosity about the damage and the injuries sustained. Another was a tall, strongly built young man. He was kind too. I think he told me he was a soldier on leave. The knees of his trousers were soaked with blood. Both of them said to me on separate occasions as I sat on the verge that I was very lucky to be alive. I recall the young man's precise words – 'If you were a cat, I'd say you've used up eight of your lives.'

The police and emergency services were on the scene by now, and I have an impression of a great many people milling about – paramedics, policemen, firemen and at least one camera crew. They all seemed hyperactive, particularly the camera crew. As I sat on the verge, I was approached by PC Paul Martin, the policeman who later became the main investigating officer for the case. He took details about my driving licence, insurance, address and the like. Martin was small and wiry, and he looked faintly incongruous in a policeman's cap that seemed too large for him. He was perfectly civil, but I felt there was an officious brusqueness and barely concealed hostility about him that put me on my guard.

I was the last of those involved in the accident to leave the scene. I had begun to develop chest pains and was taken by ambulance to Kingsmill Hospital in Mansfield. Just before I left, Martin came along and breathalysed me. I knew I was stone cold sober, but I still felt a stab of fear. Perhaps you always do when you're breathalysed – you can't escape a paranoid anxiety that the apparatus is faulty or rigged. After I had blown into it, Martin held it up in front of me. The digital display was showing a large red letter P, and he remarked, 'As you can see, the letter shows that you have passed the breathalyser test.' Phew! For a moment, I had feared that P was for 'positive'. It flashed across my mind that it could also have been for 'pissed', but I didn't say so – which is probably just as well.

A few minutes later, in the ambulance, the paramedic told me that the accident had caused three deaths. The way he put it was: 'Now that we have left the scene, I can tell you that three people did not survive the accident.' That must be the standard formula. The three who died had all been travelling south: the driver of the car lying closest to the overturned lorry, Martin Parker, and a young couple in the other car, Darren Kempton and Jennifer Lancaster, who was pregnant. The lorry driver, William Donohoe, was in a very poor condition and had been taken to hospital. He eventually recovered.

As for me, I was released from hospital after an hour or two. An ECG showed that there was no problem with my heart. All I had was bruising from my seat belt and whiplash injuries to my neck. I played down my injuries because I was anxious to get out of the hospital. I need not have worried. The medical staff were very kind, as the paramedics in the ambulance had been, but they were as eager to hasten my departure as I was, and my feet hardly touched the ground. The pains in my chest took a month or two to disappear. The neck pains took longer, but eventually passed. I had been extraordinarily lucky to escape with such minor injuries.

Those who would like to see the three people who died that day fully avenged will doubtless say that the devil's children have the devil's luck. In general, until then I had enjoyed a lucky life; perhaps one could even say a privileged one. I've been described in the press as a 'model citizen' and as 'middle class and respectable'. I concede 'middle class', but I've never thought of myself as 'respectable'. Both that word and the term 'model citizen' suggest something more prissy and moralistic than I've ever aspired to. Perhaps the right word is 'sheltered' – sheltered from deprivation, crime and sudden death.

Yes, it had been a sheltered life and things had been going quite well for me. I was in the prime of life, fifty-one years old. I was happy with my partner, Jannie, with whom I had lived for the previous seven years. I had a good relationship with my two sons from my first marriage, David and Sam. I'm a historian by trade and had taught Scandinavian history in the Department of Scandinavian Studies at University College London for almost a quarter of a century. A few years earlier, I had been promoted to senior lecturer and at the time of the accident I had served eighteen months of a five-year term as the head of my department. The headship involved a fair amount of routine paperwork, a lot of stress and occasional unpleasantness, but I found it a rewarding and creative job too. A research project which I had been working on for some years was also starting to come together. A couple of substantial articles had already emerged and I could see the contours of a book based on this research falling into place. It was this project that had put me on the road that day, since some of the archival material I needed to consult was located at Leeds.

At three or four in the afternoon, I found myself standing outside Kingsmill Hospital with the luggage from the boot of my now highly defunct car, waiting for a cab to take me to Mansfield railway station. I had to decide whether to go on to Leeds by train or to return to London. I chose to go to Leeds, which involved a tortuous train journey from Mansfield to Leeds with changes at Nottingham and Grantham. In retrospect, it was a bizarre thing to have done, but I was still very dazed at the time and I was not thinking rationally. I would certainly have gone back to London if Jannie had been there, but she was away on a research trip too, in her case abroad. She was not due to return until the following Sunday, and I didn't want to abort her visit.

But the decision was, of course, a form of denial. I was not at all clear at that point about what had happened. I was aware, though, that I had lost control of my car and caused the initial collision with the lorry, even if I was not yet certain how or why. That night in my hotel room in Leeds, I was still numb and dazed, but my mind was a cauldron of bewildered thoughts. I was wracked with muscular pain and also with guilt over the three deaths that had occurred, saying over and over to myself, 'I've killed three people, I've killed three people.'

I vaguely realised that there might be legal consequences, though it never occurred to me at that stage
that they could include prison. I had not even begun to
contemplate the possibility that the course of my future
life had been irrevocably changed, and that in my own
eyes the next eighteen months would become a struggle
to survive – and sometimes also to preserve my own
sanity.

Chapter Two
Chesterfield

In those first weeks after the accident, the sense of guilt was overpowering and prompted the most irrational thoughts. I often felt that I needed to atone somehow for my moment of error by living a better and more useful life in the future. I was responsible, yet I had escaped virtually unscathed, while three innocent people had died. I've been an agnostic since my early teens, and I have lived my whole adult life according to the principle of rationalism, so it would be incorrect to say that I felt that 'God has spared me for a purpose.' Yet there was something quasi-religious in my belief that I had to justify my survival by my future way of life.

It was combined with a desolate sense that my own life was of no value and that it would have been so much better if I had died instead of those who did. As I was to blame, it would clearly have been fairer if I, and I alone

– if anyone at all – had been killed, but the accompanying sense of my own worthlessness was self-evidently irrational. I can see now that for many weeks after the accident I was also in shock and that this contributed to the confused maelstrom of ideas.

I spent four nights in Leeds. Those days have a dream-like quality. I did some work in the archives, and that did spasmodically help to take my mind off the accident, but I couldn't think about much else for long.

A week or two later, back in London, I remembered that I had at some point reached for my jacket and that this action had led to a loss of control which had caused the initial collision with the lorry, but I believed that I had already entered the middle lane when this occurred. I was blocking out the veer to the right – to correct the drift towards the middle lane – and the terror of the central barrier rushing towards me and my second, fatal turn to left. These memories only returned after about a month.

***

In the days following the accident, I realised that I would at some point have to give a statement to the Chesterfield traffic police, but I was still too obsessed with the horrors of the accident and its consequences for the realities of my legal position to impinge on my consciousness. That changed on Saturday, 15 April, the day after I returned from Leeds, when I received through the post a so-called 'Notice of intended prosecution' from the Derbyshire Constabulary, which said that the question of prosecuting me for one of the following offences was under consideration – causing death by dangerous driving; driving without due care and attention; and driving without reasonable consideration for other persons using the road. The letter scared the wits out of me. Until that time, I had been vaguely aware that drivers were prosecuted for motoring offences, but I had never seen them listed with such precision. In particular, 'causing death by dangerous driving' sounded pretty hairy.

The following week, my insurers, Link Insurance, appointed a solicitor, Alan Hannah, to represent me. Everyone likes to slag off insurance companies, but I have to say that Terry Garland, who handled my case at Link, was extremely supportive over the next fifteen months and that Link never quibbled about the cost of my defence. I had my first meeting with Alan on 19 April and I saw him several times after that before we went up to Chesterfield to give my statement on 17 May. It took many months before we were fully at ease with each other, but I liked Alan from the start and appreciated his lack of pomposity.

As full memory of what had happened returned to me, I confronted the question of what I should say in my statement to the police. I knew from Alan that if convicted of causing death by dangerous driving, imprisonment was virtually automatic. He spoke in terms of three to six months. That was not a long sentence in the broader scheme of things, but I found the prospect of any term of imprisonment, however short, quite paralysing. I had lived my whole adult life on the assumption that I was a law-abiding citizen and would never, could never, be sent to prison. The immediate psychological effect was devastating. As I saw things then, imprisonment, even for a few months, would mean that my life was over as surely as if I had died in the accident, and I dismissed the idea that I could enjoy any sort of meaningful existence again after my release.

The burden of guilt, my sense of moral responsibility for the three deaths, became – and remains – quite detached from anything that happened as part of the legal process. I was astonished to discover that it was even possible to go to prison in this country for the sort of momentary error I had made. I felt immediately and instinctively that imprisonment would be unjust, and I have never wavered in that view – not then and not now. It followed that I did not feel any moral obligation to cut my own throat when I considered what to put into my statement to the police.

The law gave me a right to silence, and for some weeks I clung to the hope that I could exercise it. Let the bastards prove what they could prove – I didn't have to help them. I was clutching at straws. There really was no alternative. Only the truth could serve me. There was no way round the fact that I had veered into the lorry and caused the initial collision. There were plenty of other drivers in the northbound carriageway who could give evidence to that effect. If I offered no explanation, Alan was sure the court would conclude that I had fallen asleep at the wheel and that would be worse than the truth.

But on the other hand... A frank admission of the facts meant passing the point of no return. Once I had done that, I was condemned by my own words and I found the notion of assisting in my imprisonment unendurable. Alan ultimately coaxed me into accepting reality – a full and truthful statement was unavoidable and even represented my only slim chance of staying out of prison.

**

Just a week before we were due to go to Chesterfield, on

9 May, I learnt from Alan that by a strange coincidence the Highways Agency had been videotaping the flow of traffic on the stretch of motorway where the collision between my car and the lorry occurred. As it happened, the Highways Agency car was just behind us when the collision took place. The tape had been deposited at Chesterfield police station on 11 April, the day after the accident. The pictures on the tape of the interior of my car as I drifted to the left while reaching for my jacket were apparently of good quality and definition. The police had not yet disclosed this information to us, but – as Alan told me – someone at Chesterfield police station had leaked it to a local representative of Link Insurance.

What was going on? PC Martin had been in touch with me by phone a number of times since the accident. In contrast to his manner at the scene of the accident, his tone could not have been more solicitous and obliging. He was interested in my health and frightfully soothing after I received the notice of intended prosecution. It was merely precautionary, he said. By law, the police had to give notice within fourteen days of an intended prosecution for traffic offences, but that did not necessarily mean that there would be a prosecution. He had urged me to 'Try not to worry'. As I would later learn, the police were already in possession of the videotape when these telephone conversations took place.

I don't know how far Martin was acting on his own initiative in his dealings with me or whether he was following the instructions of more senior officers. He struck me as very young, so I assumed the latter at the time. Either way, I thought in those first weeks after the accident that the Chesterfield police were trying to gain my trust. They would have checked me out and known that I didn't have any sort of record. Perhaps, I thought, they hoped that a middle-class professional man would regard the police as being on his side, would see their primary social function as being to keep the lower orders at a safe distance from his property and person, and imagined that I would confide in them if approached with soft words.

If so, it was clumsy, and the police had chosen the wrong messenger. The contrast between Martin's manner at the scene of the accident and over the phone was too striking. Martin was trying to combine the roles of nasty and nice policeman (manpower shortage?), but he had come too close to nasty policeman at the scene of the accident to transmogrify easily into nice policeman. The effect was to put me somewhat on my guard, though I tried hard not to show it.

The news about the videotape showed that I had completely misunderstood what the police were doing.

Since the video had been lodged at Chesterfield police station on 11 April, they had had enough evidence to prosecute me for causing death by dangerous driving, but they had clearly not wanted me to know that. By implying that they were sympathetic and understanding. they were trying to find out what I would say. Their tactics were to see if I would make a mendacious state-ment. If I did, I would then be shown the video and forced into a series of embarrassing admissions over the points where the video contradicted my statement. The effect would be to make me look like a liar and this, in its turn, would make a jury more likely to convict in the event of a contested trial. It would also make a judge more inclined to impose a harsh sentence on me.

The police, in other words, were not solely interested in the evidence my statement might contain. In retro-spect, I can – sort of – see their point of view. Their suc-cess is measured by their conviction rate, and they were understandably trying to improve the odds of getting a conviction in my case. They were being devious, but it was not as if they were fabricating evidence. They were laying a trap, but all I had to do to avoid it was to tell the truth. I was only getting the same treatment that many routine suspects from 'the criminal classes' receive every day. All the same, I was shocked at the time – yet another reflection of the sheltered life I had led. And even now, long after the event, I feel there is an element of slipperiness in this kind of tactics which honourable men and women would find distasteful.

Back in May 2000, of course, the motives of the Chesterfield police were of no importance. What mattered was how I should react to their tactics. Alan thought we could outmanoeuvre them. I would go to Chesterfield and make a full and frank statement. Once it was made, I would decline to answer any further questions. The official transcript of my interview would therefore contain nothing of substance beyond my statement. Under this strategy, we would turn the tables on the police. We would get a truthful admission of the facts on record, block any further questioning and demonstrate that the video merely confirmed my evidence. In this way, the defence would be able to win its first skirmish with the forces of the British state.

I accepted that this was the best way to proceed, and a day or two later Alan phoned Martin again. On this occasion, when directly challenged, Martin was forced to admit what the video contained. It was agreed that Alan would be allowed to look at the video when we came to Chesterfield, while I waited outside. I would then be given a few minutes with him before

I was allowed to see the video, but only once, and the questioning would then commence.

***

On Wednesday 17 May, the interview in Chesterfield took place. I had to remain for at least half an hour in the reception area of the police station while Alan was shown the video – about seven or eight times, he told me later. Alan and I then had a consultation for about another half hour while he told me what he had seen. It was clear that the video was consistent with my recollection of events. I decided that I would not watch the video – I knew what was on it and seeing it could only upset me.

The interview then took place in a very narrow, dingy room without windows. Apart from Martin, Alan and me, the only person present was Martin's superior, a temporary inspector, who said virtually nothing. The interview was tape-recorded by the police – with one copy for them and another for Alan. After Martin asked me his first question, I merely replied that I wished to make a statement, put on my reading glasses and began. I started by saying that 'I accept that I caused the accident' and went on to give a complete and truthful account of what had happened.

This factual part of my statement was largely written by Alan on the basis of what I had told him. The last section of the statement contained what lawyers call an 'expression of contrition'. I wrote those sentences myself. They read,

> Not a day has passed since [the accident] when I have not been haunted by the thought of those poor people whose lives were cut short or who were injured and by the thought of the emotional suffering of their families. I am constantly tormented by the thought that any action of mine may have caused or contributed to those deaths and injuries.

Those words were heartfelt, but I also regarded my feelings as a private matter and no business of the police, and it had taken some persuasion from Alan for me to accept that I had to include them in my statement. That was another indication of the difficulties I was having in adjusting to the realities of my position – denial yet again. When the legal system has you in its rifle sights, there is no room left for pride.

When I had finished, I said that I did not want to say anything more, and that was it. The formal interview ended with Martin telling me that I was being 'reported' on three counts of causing death by dangerous driving. I am still not clear how 'reported' differs from 'charged' – or if it does at all. I asked when the trial was likely to be, and his superior told me that I would first be summonsed to a magistrate's court in Derbyshire, which would refer the case to the crown court. The trial would probably be held in the autumn, but the date might slip back into the early part of the following year.

After that, I was taken down to the cells in the basement to be fingerprinted and photographed. I was never quite clear whether the police had a right to do this, but Alan said that it was a quid pro quo for my not being required to come up to Chesterfield once a month to report in, as it were, during the period before my trial. When we left the police station, Martin showed us out, shook our hands and said to me, 'I am very sorry that we have had to meet under these circumstances. I know I've said this before, but try not to worry too much.' I shook Martin's hand when he offered it, but I've always regretted it. I have never seen him or had any direct contact with him since.

I remember feeling a great sense of relief at getting out of the police station. Alan told me that I had done very well in the interview. He was cock-a-hoop at how our tactics had worked, and said of Martin, 'We've spoiled his day.' Alan always remained very bitter towards Martin because of his initial failure to reveal what was on the video – far more than I was.

On the train back to London, I was drained and exhausted. I could see that we had made the best of a bad job. The police held all the cards, but we had played a bad hand well. They had the video and that was enough to convict me by itself. What Alan and I had done was damage limitation. We had produced a situation where I could not plausibly be accused of lying and that could only stand me in good stead with a judge and jury.

I knew all that and could see that there had been no real choice, but I was deeply depressed on the train. Until the interview at Chesterfield, there had still been hope, however irrational, however unrealistic. I could still toy with the notion that some *deus ex machina* would rescue me. The die was now cast and fantasies about exercising my right to silence were no longer possible. The mechanisms of state power had been cranked into life and pointed at me. I was on a road that would probably end with my imprisonment.

In retrospect, I can see that coming clean was not only the right thing to do legally. It was also the right thing to do psychologically. It meant that over the long months ahead there was no skeleton in my closet, nothing more that could come out. That knowledge was an enormous weight off my mind.

Now all I could do was to await my trial. Even in my bleakest moments, I had no idea just how long I would have to wait.

Chapter Three
The receiving end of the law

In the five or six weeks following the accident, I had learnt something about how the police operate. Over the next fourteen months, I would get some insights into the nature of the law and how the legal system works in Britain. It was a rude awakening, and in retrospect I am ashamed that I had lived my sheltered, comfortable life for so many years in uncaring ignorance of how the British state treats those it regards as 'the criminal classes'.

After Chesterfield, I assumed that my trial would probably take place sometime between October and December 2000, and that was also Alan's opinion. But through that long summer there wasn't a squeak from the police or the CPS, the Crown Prosecution Service. The summons to appear at 10 a.m. on 19 October at Ilkeston Magistrate's Court to answer the charge of causing death by dangerous driving only hit my doormat on 30 September, even though it was dated 29 August. I never discovered why the summons took a month to reach me. The hearing was later adjourned for almost a month and I did not appear before Ilkeston Magistrate's Court until 16 November.

The proceedings took less than five minutes. I merely had to confirm my name and address, and I was then unconditionally bailed to appear in Derby Crown Court on 12 January 2001. I was not asked to enter a plea to the charge.

As it turned out, the hearing on 12 January never took place. The CPS were so slow in sending some of their evidence to the defence that the hearing had to be rescheduled for 5 February. That in its turn was cancelled when the court learnt that there would be a contested trial. I assumed that we were only facing a delay until March at worst, and so did my lawyers. Some chance! A few weeks later, I was informed that my trial would be held at Derby Crown Court on Monday, 23 July. My unconditional bail was extended until that date.

The upshot was that I had to wait fourteen months between my interview with the police in May 2000 and my trial in July 2001. Fourteen months of uncertainty over my fate, fourteen months of mental torment for me and my family. If I had to rank the punishments I have suffered as a result of that fatal misjudgement I made behind the driving wheel on 10 April 2000, I would place those fourteen months near the top of the list. It was the cruellest punishment, and it was inflicted on the basis of allegation alone before I had been convicted of any offence.

The delay in bringing me to trial was somewhat longer than normal in the case of a motoring offence, but is no way unusual. In prison, I would meet men who had waited years for trial and not always on unconditional bail. The entitlement to reasonably swift justice ought to be a fundamental human right. Yes, some charges are highly complex and it takes time for the prosecution to prepare for trial, but the real explanation for most of the delays in bringing cases to trial is our old friend, 'lack of resources', in the shape of courtroom time. The British state is keen to prosecute, but less interested in providing enough magistrates, judges and courthouses.

It is an attitude that could only be justified by the belief that anyone who has been accused of a criminal offence belongs to a sub-human species undeserving of the slightest compassion or consideration. That is a belief that goes against one of the most basic principles of British law, the presumption of innocence until conviction has been secured, and yet it is the belief on which the British state is allowed to operate in practice. That is a disgrace.

***

This was my first lesson in the law. There were more to come, and they commenced at my first 'conference' with a barrister, Roger Bedford (not his real name), on 20 July, at which Jannie and Alan were also present. It was very much a preliminary meeting as we had nothing to go on beyond my statement and Alan's recollection of what he had seen on the video. Roger was flash as a rat with a gold tooth. Tall and fair, with sharp, beaky features, he was wearing a dark suit in the summer heat with a loud tie and matching breast pocket handkerchief and prominent gold cufflinks. He was almost standing to attention when we came in. He made me think of an exclamation mark. His greeting was very courteous, but there was a slight quasi-military bark in his voice. I surmised that he would doubtless have quite an imposing courtroom presence.

Roger went through extracts from *Wilkinson's Road Traffic Offences*, the main authority on motoring law, and various recent cases of causing death by dangerous driving. He stressed that he could not give me definitive advice until he had seen the outline of the prosecution case, but I got the strong impression that he considered me guilty of causing death by dangerous driving and that he believed a jury would find against me if there were a contested trial. The jury would be prejudiced against me, because three people, including a pregnant woman, had died. My only slim chance would lie in a good performance in the witness box. The whole thrust of Roger's remarks was that I ought to plead guilty and he was very emphatic about the benefits of doing so. What he called 'the discount' for a guilty plea was, he claimed, one third to one half off one's sentence. A plea of guilty, mitigation laid on with a trowel, a short prison sentence and then, in his quaint phrase, 'we can all get on with our lives again'. This made imprisonment sound like going into hospital for a hernia operation.

This was not very different from what Alan had been telling me over the previous two months, but the bomb-shell lay in what Roger had to say about sentencing. The climate was becoming more severe, non-custodial sentences for causing death by dangerous driving ever more rare and prison sentences ever more harsh. In his opinion, I would get six to eighteen months if I pleaded guilty, eighteen to thirty-six or perhaps even forty-two months if I pleaded not guilty and was then convicted by the jury. I had learnt by now that for sentences under four years, a prisoner was automatically released halfway through his sentence and could get up to an additional two months off with Home Detention Curfew (electronic tagging). He was therefore talking about sentences which stretched in terms of time served from a few months at best to more than a year and a half at worst.

This was a lot worse than anything I had heard before and scared the wits out of me – even though Alan told me later that he personally stuck to his former opinion that a sentence in the region of three to six months was likely. The only chink of light was Roger's remark that there was 'a less than ten per cent chance' that I would receive a non-custodial sentence on a guilty plea. 'I know judges who wouldn't send you to prison,' he said, but they were a minority.

My conference with Roger had given me a lot of food for thought. He had been very persuasive. I was impressed by him but also infuriated by what I perceived as his attempt to frighten me into a guilty plea with the spectre of ordeal by cross-examination and a longer sentence, if I lost a contested trial. With the benefit of distance, I'm sure that Roger was looking out for my best interests, and he did stress that the decision was mine and that he would do his very best for me if I chose to plead not guilty. But at the time, I got the impression that I was totally alone, engaged in a hopeless struggle against the entire legal system. The whole process seemed designed to deliver me at the prison gates like a trussed turkey with a minimum of fuss or bother.

The thing that struck me most forcefully in my meeting with Roger were his remarks about 'the discount'. Many people have told me that the motivation behind the discount is purely pragmatic – it saves government money by saving court time. I'm sure that's true, but I suspect there are additional elements. British sentencing practice was shaped by Christian judges convinced that sinners who repented and confessed their sin were superior to sinners who didn't. The discount is also highly convenient to the state in that it will often secure a prosecution victory without the risk of defeat that always attends a jury trial.

I was outraged by the discount, but also as intimidated by it as you are meant to be. I came away from the meeting with Roger convinced that I would be crazy to do anything other than plead guilty. The risk of a sentence that might keep me in prison for something like twenty months was simply too terrifying to contemplate. I accepted that the only course was to plead guilty and throw myself on the mercy of the court, bleating about my good character and my previous unblemished driving record.

The discount is the most pernicious aspect of the

British system of criminal justice, and it has little in common with the American system of open and explicit plea-bargaining. I was just high enough up the socio-intellectual food chain to consider disregarding legal advice. But when I think about the effect the discount had on me, there is no difficulty in seeing how it is cynically exploited to bully frightened, badly educated young boys into abandoning their right to trial.

**

For the moment, my conference with Roger had left me scared and beaten into submission. Even so, I did now begin to read about Britain's motoring laws in a serious way for the first time. Roger had given me photocopies of the relevant parts of *Wilkinson* (don't ask me who Wilkinson is or was) and summaries of a number of recent cases that had come before the court of appeal. Over the following months, Alan sent me more cases of this kind and I also kept an eye on the press for court reports involving driving offences.

I'm not a lawyer and I'm sure that large gaps in my understanding remain, but I quickly became convinced that our current motoring laws are profoundly confused. I was being charged with causing death by dangerous driving. This is the supreme motoring offence, punishable by up to ten years in prison. The next step down is simple 'dangerous driving' – that's to say, equally bad driving that does not involve fatalities. The maximum sentence is two years in prison. After that comes 'driving without due care and attention', which is generally referred to by the convenient shorthand of 'careless driving'. You can't be sent to prison for careless driving: a fine of up to £2,500 and a driving ban are as bad as it can get.

I have three difficulties with this range of offences and penalties. The first is the very existence of a crime called 'causing death by dangerous driving' and the yawning gap between the maximum sentences for that offence and for simple 'dangerous driving'. I have no problem with ten years, or even longer, as a maximum sentence for driving offences. There are clearly cases where the behaviour of a motorist is so reprehensible that sentences in this kind of range might be justified.

What I could not see was the justice of a separate offence, namely causing death by dangerous driving, that is defined only by its consequences. What is the court supposed to punish? The negligent driving or the deaths that it causes? Both obviously, but how does the court strike the right balance between the two when pure chance alone will usually determine whether an act of dangerous driving causes death or not. The dilemma can never be resolved so long as this offence continues to exist on the statute book.

My second difficulty with our motoring laws relates to the distinction between dangerous and careless driving. I read through the relevant sections of *Wilkinson* with growing incredulity. Roger had kept emphasising at our conference that the distinction was meant to be an objective one. That is precisely what it is not. The distinction between dangerous and careless driving is in fact nebulous and subjective – all it amounts to is an assumed difference between driving that is *far below* and *below* respectively the standard of a prudent driver. On that alleged distinction rests the liberty of the accused.

The obvious question is 'how far is far?' Perhaps our old mate, *Wilkinson*, can help us to answer this question. *Wilkinson* gives examples of careless driving under two headings. The first is 'acts ... caused by more than momentary inattention', for example, overtaking on the inside, driving too close to another vehicle and driving through a red light. The second is 'conduct which clearly caused the driver not to be in a position to respond in the event of an emergency on the road', for example, using a mobile, tuning a car radio, reading a map, selecting and lighting a cigarette.

Wilkinson adds that these examples might explain, for example, why a driver veered across a carriageway.

This sounds fairly broad and might suggest that momentary inattention comes under the category of careless driving. Not so fast! *Wilkinson* goes on to say that the examples are listed merely 'because *usually* when this conduct occurs the appropriate charge will be' careless driving. However, in such cases,

> ...it is necessary to go beyond the explanation for the driving and consider whether the particular facts of the case warrant a charge of careless or dangerous driving. The reason for the driver's behaviour is not relevant to the choice of charge: it is the acts of driving which determine whether [it is careless or dangerous driving]... Police officers and prosecutors must always consider the manner of the driving in the context of the other facts in the case to decide the most appropriate way forward.

These last two sentences struck me as gobbledegook (the penultimate one beginning 'The reason for ...' is a particularly ripe and oozy piece of impenetrable prose), but I think they mean that an action may be careless in one set of circumstances, but is dangerous in another.

The outcome of my reading was to leave me uncertain as to whether I was guilty of dangerous or careless driving. I remain uncertain to this day. The mistake I made seems on the face of it to fall into the kinds of error *Wilkinson* lists as careless driving, so it's all a matter of whether 'the particular facts of the case' pushed it into the category of dangerous driving. The real scandal is that neither I nor anyone else can be absolutely sure. *Wilkinson* claims that some of the changes made in 1988 and 1991 to British motoring law were designed to address 'the lack of any sufficiently established distinction' between dangerous and careless driving. Well, if that's the case, all I can say to our lawmakers is – keep trying, boys and girls, because you haven't made it yet.

My bafflement was not lessened by some of the cases I studied. Juries do sometimes acquit motorists charged with causing death by dangerous driving, even when the driving was extremely poor – far worse than mine had been. When I've pressed lawyers about apparent anomalies like this, the reply has usually been along the lines, 'Oh well, you know, juries can do anything, you might as well roll dice.' I don't think this is entirely fair to juries in motoring cases. Perhaps the problem is not merely the fickleness of juries, but the ambiguous nature of the distinction between dangerous and careless driving. It is that ambiguity more than anything else that injects an element of playing roulette into the proceedings.

In the last resort, of course, I didn't care a fig whether my driving was called dangerous or careless so long as I didn't go to prison. This brings me to my third difficulty with the current legal framework surrounding motoring offences: sentencing practice. Roger was right and everything I read after our conference supported his view on this point – imprisonment has become the standard, almost invariable penalty for causing death by dangerous driving, though the odd non-custodial sentence is still occasionally imposed.

I presume that current sentencing practice for causing death by dangerous driving rests in part at least on some notion of what we might call 'adequate retribution' – a moral conviction that negligence must be punished by prison when it leads to death. Moral perceptions naturally differ, but I do not find it morally self-evident that negligence which causes death must always lead to imprisonment regardless of individual circumstances. I believe that my case illustrates the point, and I'm sure that there are others that do too.

There is obviously no excuse for the error of judgment I made, but my remorse and grief over the three deaths that occurred has never made me feel that imprisonment was a just or appropriate punishment. I felt this way because of my circumstances. My misjudgment was momentary, lasting a few seconds. I was not under the influence of drink or drugs. I was not speeding. I had held a driving licence for almost twenty years. In that time, I had never been charged, let alone convicted, of any driving offence (or other offence, for that matter) and I had never been involved in a motor accident of any kind.

There are many cases where a custodial sentence should be imposed for driving offences. I have little sympathy for drivers who are drunk or drugged, drivers who race at high speed against other drivers, motorists who drive recklessly for prolonged periods of time and drivers who grossly exceed the speed limit. In such cases, a custodial sentence may well be the right one, especially when there are prior convictions. But what I cannot do is to accept that my behaviour is comparable to theirs and that we should all be lumped together under the all-purpose heading of 'killer drivers'.

In my ruminations, I did also consider the question of deterrence and the feelings of the bereaved. The deterrence argument is always brought out for a quick canter round the paddock when imprisonment needs to be defended. There would be some point, if not much justice, in jailing drivers for a momentary error if it saved life.

But common sense and everyday observation tell us that we do not make a link between the driving of accused motorists and our own driving. We all look up from the newspaper and say to ourselves, 'What an idiot! I'd never do anything like that.' And then we go and do it – or something similar.

It is possible that harsh sentences have a deterrent effect in relation to drink-driving, but no motorist will drive more carefully himself because he reads of an example of imprisonment for momentary misjudgement or inattention. The reason is simple – the capacity for momentary misjudgement or inattention is innate to all human beings, and that applies behind a driving wheel as it does everywhere else. Imposing the occasional 'exemplary' prison sentence when opportunity, in the form of evidence, presents itself will not change that. This is not to diminish my own culpability. It is to state the obvious.

Finally, there was the matter of the bereaved, and I did give this a lot of thought. I accept as a general principle that a civilised society can only rest on the assumption that individuals will refrain from private acts of vengeance. This means that the state must inflict a sufficient level of retribution to appease victims and their families. The problem is that, when people have died in a motor accident, rather than as a result of intentional crime, the courts will often be unable to satisfy their families.

This point was made rather well by the appeal court in 1995 when dismissing an appeal against sentence by the Attorney-General in the case of a motorist who was convicted of causing death by dangerous driving, but spared imprisonment. The judges observed that 'even if a short sentence of imprisonment is imposed, those who are closely related to the victim will feel that it is an inadequate measure of the loss of life'. And why was that? It was because the court must 'approach the case very much with the offending in mind and *the degree of criminality involved*' (my italics). There's the nub and the rub. In motoring cases, the courts can never function mechanically as a mere device for exacting retribution. The need to assuage the bereaved cannot override the fundamental demand on any legal system for fairness, for a sentencing policy that takes into account 'the degree of criminality involved'.

The reading and thinking I did about the motoring laws during those months in the late summer and early autumn of 2000 left me incensed at their illogicality. I formed the view then, which I still hold, that both the offence of causing death by dangerous driving and the absurd distinction between dangerous and careless driving should be abolished. They should be replaced by a single offence, which might perhaps be called negligent driving, that is subject to a more graduated and flexible scale of penalties. Some cases of bad driving are obviously worse than others, but this can be dealt with through sentencing. If we had one charge and allowed sentencing to rest on a painstaking examination of the circumstances of each case, we could make the claim that we had rational motoring laws.

Gaining some understanding of the motoring laws and sentencing practice did not do me any immediate good. They merely added anger and outrage to the terror of prison that I already felt. But the discount doth make cowards of us all, and for the time being I remained paralysed by it. All my instincts rebelled against the course on which I was set. I thought it morally wrong to plead guilty when I was not convinced of my own guilt or to connive in my own imprisonment by a guilty plea when I felt my imprisonment would be unjust.

My inner voice told me to fight, but my reason whispered 'surrender' and that was still what I assumed I would do. Virtually all the mitigating factors (no previous convictions, a clean driving record etc.) were on my side, and even the pessimistic Roger Bedford thought that my statement to the police 'read well'. So all common sense screamed out – go for it! Plead guilty and let a silvery-tongued barrister pile on the mitigation with a fork-lift truck. And above all get the discount off the prison sentence! But I remained hesitant, and it would take many months of agonising before I reached a resolution.

Chapter Four
Listening to the inner voice

The summons I received on 30 September 2000 had promised 'an outline' of the prosecution case. An 'outline' doesn't sound like much, but in fact the term covers all the evidence at the disposal of the prosecution. The CPS proved in no hurry to supply it. On 20 October Alan sent me the witness statements, and three weeks later, the famous video, which I did finally force myself to watch – a grim but necessary experience. Many of the pages of the witness statements were missing (largely because it had not occurred to the person photocopying them that many pages had writing on both sides) and the CPS had to be chased to send them. The last piece of prosecution evidence reached us on 29 December.

As the evidence dribbled through from the CPS, I continued to agonise over the plea I would enter. I came to incline increasingly towards a plea of not guilty and decided to seek a second opinion from another barrister. Alan arranged for me to see Stephen Brown (once again not his real name), and I met him at his chambers on the evening of 29 November. He was very different from Roger Bedford in both appearance and personality. He was quite stout with a bizarre haircut – short back and sides but surmounted by a frizzled crew cut, perhaps intended to make the wearing of wig in court more comfortable. Where Bedford had been imperious and disdainful, Brown was soft and ingratiating, his legal observations attended by frequent clenched grins and jokes.

Brown had taken a lot of trouble. He had showed the video and my statement to many of his colleagues – with the interesting result that some thought my driving careless, others dangerous. Brown clearly belonged to the second camp. Even so, he believed a plea of not guilty 'will run', as he put it, but he thought that I would only win with three juries in every ten. The prosecution had an easy job. 'They just need to keep showing the video to the jury' – and they would find endless excuses to do so. On the other hand, he did stress that a plea of not guilty represented my only real chance of staying out of prison – only victory in a contested trial would spare me a custodial sentence. On a plea of guilty, he thought that a sentence 'towards the lenient end of the scale' was likely, say twelve to eighteen months.

There was probably not a judge in the country (or even the prosecution), he claimed, who would want to send me to prison, but all judges would do so for two reasons. The first was how a non-custodial sentence would be presented in the tabloids the next day – 'Judge lets off one of us'. This represented a view of the social status of university teachers which I found a little curious – power grows out of the barrel of a chequebook, and we academics have a short purse. The second was that whoever presided at my trial would be worried that leniency in my case would be yet more grist to the mill of politicians who wanted to interfere with the sentencing powers of judges.

All of this was accompanied by a series of jokes, most snobbish, all in doubtful taste. On the question of juries and how different they can be, he remarked that if you got a jury recruited from a council estate, they were unlikely to 'regard stabbing as a crime, unless it led to death', whereas juries from 'a nice part of Kent' would consider burglary the most serious offence imaginable. As for the new, more severe climate of opinion about offences like my own, he would have told clients twelve or fifteen years ago, 'Don't worry about prison, just turn up at the court, but bring your chequebook.'

For the time being, Stephen had pushed me back towards a guilty plea. He had essentially said the same thing as Roger Bedford, and it seemed mad to go against the advice of two barristers. The only rational course was to plead guilty and place my hopes in the more lenient sentence that was supposed to produce. It went against all my instincts, but I stuck to that view for the next three weeks or so.

In the end, I couldn't go through with it. Above all, it was my inner voice. I simply felt that my imprisonment would be wrong, and I could not bring myself to connive in it, to surrender my liberty without a fight. I did not think I was going to win – I accepted what Roger Bedford and Stephen Brown had said about my chances of victory. My not guilty plea was intended mainly as a gesture of defiance, and I expected to pay a price for that in the form of a harsher sentence.

I had made up my mind, but I still felt I should give Alan a chance to persuade me if he wanted to, so I invited him to meet me informally for a drink on 20 December. I expected what they call 'robust discussion', but it transpired that Alan – who, of course, could guess what was going through my head – had clearly come to the same conclusion as me. In fact, he mentioned an additional argument against pleading guilty – that I would for the rest of my life have a nagging doubt in my mind that I might have avoided prison if I had decided to fight the charge.

After that, things moved quickly in the next couple of days. Alan found me a new barrister in the form of Annette Henry, who agreed with our decision to plead not guilty. (I give her real name as the fact that she appeared for me in court is a matter of public record.) Alan admitted to me that he was very relieved by Annette's attitude, since he had felt a bit 'out on a limb' in agreeing with me to go against the views of two barristers.

The defence strategy was set out in the instructions to counsel which Alan wrote, and I read, on 29 December. The cardinal feature of the defence case was Alan's assessment, based on watching the video, that the period of my distraction while I was reaching for the jacket was about two seconds. This meant that my action 'was not a continuous course of bad driving' over a prolonged period of time. It was on this basis that Annette was asked to persuade a jury that my actions fell below, but not far below, the standard of a prudent driver. This was to be reinforced by putting to the jury the 'there but for the grace of God go I' argument – this could have happened to any ordinary driver.

Nonetheless, the tactics were to hedge our bets against the possibility of defeat by not mounting an aggressive defence. The prosecution evidence would not be challenged. It would simply be ignored so as to focus the jury on, to quote the instructions, the 'real evidence' – the video and my statement. It would not therefore be a question of 'putting witnesses through the pain or difficulty of giving evidence, or cost to the State, or to any appreciable extent of the time of the Court'. Moreover, if the jury went against me, Annette was to argue in mitigation that my full statement to the police ought to carry the same mitigatory value as a plea of guilty would have done. It had not been 'a self-serving statement' and amounted to a frank admission of fault.

There was, however, one piece of prosecution evidence that we could not accept. It was a series of photos taken at the scene of the accident which included horrific images of the victims taken after their deaths. Alan advised me not to look at them myself, and I didn't. If these photos were seen by the jury, the effect would be highly prejudicial to my case, and we would therefore seek an order from the judge to keep them from the jury. We had our way on this point. Within days the CPS had given way. They agreed to exclude not only the photos but also all other evidence, including all the witness statements, except for the video itself and my statement. This would make for a much simpler and quicker trial, exactly the sort of trial we wanted. It was a small victory, but of course the CPS still had the video and my statement. I had few illusions – I realised that in all probability that would be enough. Perhaps the photos of the victims had never been more than a try on.

On 23 January I had my first conference with Annette Henry, but there wasn't really much to say. The defence strategy was already in place and it was just a matter of waiting. Annette came across as a normal human being and did not affect the Olympian pomposities in which lawyers sometimes indulge. She was not absurdly optimistic about the likely verdict, but thought that we had a fighting chance and that I was right to plead not guilty. If she could persuade the jury that I was just an ordinary driver who made a momentary mistake, then we could win. It was no better – or worse – than that.

One further step was taken to assist my defence. Alan and Annette thought it would be a good idea to get a timed version of the video made to see if it confirmed Alan's assessment that I drifted to the left for about two seconds while reaching for my jacket. It was available in early February and placed the duration of the drift at 1.96 seconds. The timed version of the tape was submitted to the CPS and the court as the only item of defence evidence. That precise timing of 1.96 seconds would do me enormous good in shaping perceptions of my case.

And that was it until July 2001 – virtually nothing happened on the legal front after that for six months. Early in July, PC Martin resurfaced and rang Alan to ask if we would agree to postponing the trial by a few weeks because the summer holiday he had booked coincided with it. Alan took the view that we had waited long enough already for my trial and said 'no', so the evidence Martin would have given was presented at my trial by another policeman from Chesterfield.

On Friday 20 July, I had a last pre-trial conference with Annette and Alan. So little had been happening over the last six months that it was only the second time I met Annette. My trial was due to begin on the following Monday, and I was pretty jumpy by this stage. Not much emerged from the meeting, except that Annette did now hazard a speculation as to sentence. The price of defeat was likely to be 'eighteen months to two years, and could be more'. She put the chances of victory no higher than fifty-fifty.

This was not a cheery note on which to begin what could have been my last weekend of freedom for some time to come, but I had no regrets or hesitations about my plea. All the lawyers I had consulted assumed that the jury's verdict would be visceral rather than analytical. If they could be persuaded that I was just an ordinary bloke who had made a mistake like every other driver sometimes does, they might acquit. If they felt that only prison could pay the blood debt I owed, they would find me guilty.

I had plenty of reasoned arguments for pleading not guilty, but in the last resort my motives were equally emotional. They were rooted in my gut instincts. Back in October 2000, I had written in my diary that

> I will always be ashamed if I allow the fear of cross-examination and of a longer sentence to lead me down the path of surrender. I will retain my self-respect if I do battle for my survival in the witness box, even if I lose in the end.

That was the bottom line. I entered a plea of not guilty, not because I was confident I would win, but to save my soul.

Chapter Five
Holding on

I experienced the fifteen months between the accident and my trial as a period of emotional and psychological turmoil. That turmoil took many forms and its strands overlapped and intertwined, but three elements stand out – guilt, fear and alienation. The source of the first will be obvious. The primary emotional problem for any normal human being in my shoes was the remorse, the awareness that I was to blame for three deaths.

Within a couple of months of the accident, I decided that I would never drive again. I know that it is a pointless gesture of atonement which does no good to anyone. My psychotherapist, Joe (of whom more later) unsuccessfully tried to talk me out of it, arguing that I was inflicting an excessive punishment on myself. Indeed, he said, I had to think of the benefit to my family and 'society' of my owning and driving a car. I was struck by how many people regard life without a car as quite unthinkable. But I have kept to my resolution.

As it became clear that the police and the CPS were after my head, remorse had to jostle with an equally powerful emotion, the terror of prison. This may not be admirable, but it is all too human. As Joe said to me at one of our sessions, I perceived myself as fighting for survival and that would always exercise a powerful hold on the mind. I had never been to prison, I had never imagined it possible that I might one day go to prison, so fear was compounded by profound ignorance.

The little I knew from the occasional TV programme or newspaper article suggested that British prisons were antiquated and brutal. Over the summer of 2000, I tried to find out something about what life inside one of them would be like, and it was no easy task. No one seemed to know anything about it, least of all lawyers, and I received some strange and contradictory tips – some from people who had worked in prisons. My only source of any real value was the Prison Reform Trust, which was very helpful in answering my questions and sent me a copy of the *Prisoners Information Handbook*. This document is jointly produced by the Trust and the Prison Service and only contains statements that the latter is prepared to accept. You cannot consequently take everything in it seriously, but it did tell me a lot about prison regulations and different categories of prison.

What it didn't do was give me any real feel for what prison life was like. Prison was still a mysterious foreign country, and I remained terrified of my journey to its shores. Incarceration as such, the prospect of being locked away, was never my paramount fear. Nor did I ever think in terms of shame or loss of social standing. I never believed that my offence had a moral dimension and always assumed that no one I cared for or respected would hold my imprisonment against me.

From the start, what I really feared was what I called 'humiliation' and 'disempowerment'. What I meant by this was having to follow a set of oppressive rules enforced by malicious prison officers and being subjected to bullying or worse by other prisoners. I assumed that I would be victimised or at the very least viewed with hostility by both groups, because I was an educated, middle-class university teacher. And I did not think the prison officers would be any better than the prisoners – I could not see why anyone other than a sadistic pervert would want to pursue a career in the prison service. In my calmer moments, I conceded that many prison officers may have joined the service merely because they wanted a job and this was the only one going. I was also horrified by the lack of privacy, the thought of having to share a cell with someone who might be hostile or uncongenial.

I did admit to myself that I was suffering from what Christians call 'the sin of pride'. As I keep saying, I had lived a sheltered life. I was accustomed to being treated with courtesy and a measure of respect. The thought that this would change and that I would have to bow and scrape to people I despised in order to survive suffused me with an incandescent rage.

***

I've been asked several times, once on TV, whether I ever considered suicide, the ultimate exit strategy. Of course, I did. Everyone does in this kind of situation. It started the day I received the notice of intended prosecution from the police, 15 April 2000. I was never serious. It was always a fantasy, a daydream. It was a form of emotional relief to sit, particularly in the evening with a stiff scotch in my hand, and ruminate about the ancient Romans, who saw nothing as more shameful than to allow one's living body to fall into the hands of one's enemies.

Such suicidal speculations are, I imagine, fairly common among those facing imprisonment, and it is a useful psychological safety valve, a way of pretending to yourself for a few hours that there is an alternative. But, of course, it was impossible. I could never inflict such grief on my sons and above all on Jannie. Sometimes, in my moments of blackest despair, this made me angry with them – I resented them for presenting an obstacle to suicide. As Joe told me, this was 'textbook'.

What else held me back? Above all, the will to survive, the fear of death. That goes without saying. But there was also an element of defiance. I wrote in my diary in early September 2000.

> My death will give those who want to put me in jail too much satisfaction. By going on living, I will deny the bastards their ultimate triumph. And if I'm being sent to prison for the sake of vengeance, then to survive and to go on to lead a happy and successful life afterwards will be my revenge.

And, of course, there was the fact that I was not facing all that long a sentence – I regarded my stretch as 'survivable'. How I would have reacted if I had faced a sentence that would have robbed me of most of my remaining active life is another matter. Finally, there was the matter of my medical ignorance – I simply could not think of a way of taking my own life that was quick and effective without being unspeakably gruesome.

I also daydreamed about the possibility of abscondment. Once again, classical analogies came to mind – Hannibal on the run from the Romans in the eastern Mediterranean during the last years of his life, Ovid by the shores of the Black Sea. I didn't know if the offence was extraditable, but I assumed it was, so I called abscondment 'the northern Cyprus option'. Oddly enough, I always thought of flight abroad and the option of moving to, say, Liverpool and living under the name of Reilly or whatever never occurred to me, even though that must be the most common form which abscondment takes.

It was, of course, quite impractical. I still had my passport and I did indeed go abroad twice for a break while awaiting trial. But I came back without a moment's hesitation – though also with a certain wistful regret as Eurostar emerged from the Chunnel into the lush countryside of Kent. I did not have the financial resources to establish myself abroad for the rest of my life. The daydream was just another emotional safety valve.

***

My overriding reason for rejecting flight was not really money. Above all, I did not want to exile myself from

Britain, which I saw as my country. This is curious as my feelings about Britain, or perhaps I should say England, became very ambivalent during the summer and autumn of 2000. No bonds of blood and soil tied me to this country. I'm Danish by birth, but after the age of three I spent my whole childhood in Australia. In those days, the Fifties and early Sixties, Britain was presented as 'the mother country' in Australian schools. We studied English literature and British history. When I came to London at the age of nineteen to attend university, I perceived it as the centre of the universe.

I've stayed ever since, and I had gradually become very attached to England. The way of life and the people were congenial by and large. I say 'England' because in thirty-five years I've never strayed beyond London and the south-east for long. I gave up my Danish passport and became a British citizen. I never forgot that I did not have a drop of British blood in my veins, but I was happy enough to think of myself as essentially British by culture and by choice.

Some of the bitterness and anger I felt at the prospect of imprisonment was really the self-pitying wail of the discarded lover. It arose from shock that the apparatus of the British state had been turned against me, when I had loved England so deeply.

What had previously seemed quaint and charming,

now seemed arbitrary and oppressive. How English to enact a distinction between dangerous and careless driving that no one can understand and to allow the liberty of the negligent motorist to depend on jury roulette! How English to proclaim that the accused is presumed innocent and then let him twist slowly in the wind waiting for a trial that may be delayed for years! What else to expect from the country that relishes its miscarriages of justice and loves to remember the geriatric hanging judges of the golden past! Like public services that work, a legal system that failed to be capricious would derogate from England's charm. Underfunding and impenetrability rule, OK?

It was this kind of semi-rational thought-world that made one part of me want to reject Britain, to leave and never return once my sentence was over. For practical and family reasons, emigration was never really an option at my age. It was yet another psychological safety valve, a daydream to walk side by side with suicide and abscondment. In any case, I wasn't sure that I wanted – or ought – to leave. I had chosen to make Britain my home and, if I thought change was needed, perhaps I had a duty to do the what little I could to support it rather than to decamp.

This emotional seesaw was particularly intense during the last six months of 2000. After that, once I had decided to plead not guilty and had a legal team committed to that strategy, it became far less acute and I began to reconnect mentally with British society.

**

My anglophobic flights of fancy were also undermined by the knowledge that my quarrel was not with the British people, but with the law and the legal system. The ordinary people of this country, not marginal outsiders like me, have always been the first victims of the British state. It was they who faced the hangman's rope in the past and who provide the prison fodder today.

I had been very struck by one of Stephen Brown's remarks – that the judge would see me as 'one of us'. Annette made the same point at our first conference in January 2001, when she said that the judge would regard me as someone 'from his own class'. At the time, I was grossly offended. How could I be one of us? I had no wealth or power, I hadn't been to a British public school, I had no influential family contacts in this country. I was just a lackey of the ruling elite, employed to complete the education of their offspring like some eighteenth-century dancing instructor. Never 'one of us' again!

At some level, it was an impossible aspiration. I could no more reject my background and experience than I could England. Just as I could not escape the reality of having become British by language and culture, I was imprisoned by the consequences of education and lifestyle. But what I could do was to be more active in supporting not just legal reform but also radical political and social change. The general election of 2001 helped to crystallise my ideas in this respect. For some years, I had been a highly inactive member of the Labour Party, but in May 2001 I put a fair amount of effort into working for a Labour victory in the constituency where I lived. And yes, before the reader says so, let me concede that the Blair government hardly represented radicalism. But I took the view, which I still hold, that Labour was the only political force in Britain that contained the potential, however slight, for achieving any real change. That involvement in politics at the local level in the early summer of 2001 was important to me psychologically – it represented a decision to try and turn away from alienation and to make some small contribution towards supporting the forces working for greater humanity in British society.

***

In short, in addition to being totally fucked legally, I was not a in good way psychologically. To adapt Scott

Turow's memorable words, I 'had my head completely stuck up my ass'. How did I cope? In a multitude of ways, but above all because I was extremely fortunate in having the unwavering support of my family and friends. Jannie's love and loyalty were absolutely solid. We had been planning to marry for some time, but without any precise date in mind. The crisis in my affairs made us act more urgently, and the marriage took place in September 2000. My two sons, and especially the eldest, David, who was already an adult, were also a great source of comfort. Words cannot express how important they and Jannie were to me or how much I valued the support of the tiny group of personal friends, no more than half a dozen, who knew the secret of my situation.

***

I also spent a fair amount of time with shrinks one way or another. I resisted the idea of counselling at first, but eventually I saw a psychiatrist in early June 2000. He thought that I did not need to see him very often and that I should get my regular counselling from a psychotherapist, Joe Richards (not his real name).

I first met Joe on 27 June, and after that I saw him roughly once a month until my trial. Joe is a cognitive behavioural psychotherapist. What this means, he told me, was that the therapist is not just a listener. He is more proactive, so that the session becomes a discussion between the therapist and the patient. His aim is to combat 'thinking distortions', because such distortions lead to 'bad feelings about oneself'. Occasionally, the therapist plays devil's advocate in order to put another perspective to the patient.

I don't think that Joe felt I was a particularly worrying patient. He took the view that everything depends on how far you have a resilient personality, not the degree of stress to which you are subjected. In his assessment, I had a highly resilient personality and would therefore survive whatever shit was thrown at me.

I found my early sessions with Joe quite disturbing, but I got a lot out of our meetings. I needed someone to unburden myself to, someone who would listen, and I think it was helpful that this was someone who answered back and engaged in a dialogue. This interactive aspect of the cognitive behavioural approach is its greatest strength. And as Jannie pointed out, if I hadn't had Joe, she would have had to listen to my most savage and bleak reflections and taken the flak when she tried to put a more rational perspective. I let Joe answer back without becoming enraged – I wouldn't have taken it if we had not been in a counsellor/patient relationship.

***

The fear of prison had a professional dimension. If I lost my job, bankruptcy, repossession, impoverishment all moved onto the agenda and there was a risk that, given my age, I would never work again. My knowledge of employment law was just as hazy as my familiarity with motoring offences in the spring of 2000, and what I could ascertain from Alan and my union, the Association of University Teachers, was not conclusive. A term of imprisonment is apparently not in itself grounds for dismissal unless the offence is relevant to one's work. There were provisions for dismissing academics who 'brought the college into disrepute', but that could not apply, given the circumstances of my case. That left dismissal for 'non-performance of duties', and I would obviously be vulnerable to that if sent to prison for any significant length of time, since you cannot be in two places at the same time.

There were some factors working in my favour. In the summer of 2000, I was coming towards the end of my twenty-fourth year of employment at University College London, so I was approaching old-retainer status. I knew of cases where college had been extremely supportive of staff experiencing legal or other difficulties. But I had been around a long time and had also heard some ugly stories of academics who had been squeezed out. I didn't know what to expect.

The bull needed to be taken by the horns, especially since I was finding it increasingly difficult in the spring of 2000 to cope with the demands of my job. In early May I chaired an appointment committee to select a new member of staff in my department, and I remember that day as the last occasion when I felt that I was master of the situation, that I had a complete grip on events as head of department. By the time I was responsible for arrangements at a two-day international conference I had organised six weeks later, the mental effort of keeping an overview of events and making small talk to distinguished visitors was a prolonged agony. I was losing it.

By then, I knew that liberation was at hand. On 25 May I saw the Vice-Provost responsible for a cluster of faculties that included my own, Professor Michael Worton, and put him in the picture. Many people at work knew that I had been involved in a serious car accident, but the fact that I was facing criminal charges had not been reported in the press and no one at college knew about it before my meeting with Michael. I told him that, since drink or a prolonged course of reckless driving were not involved, the offence did not raise questions about my integrity and that accordingly I did not think the crisis I faced necessitated my resignation as head of department and still less as a member of academic staff. Michael replied that he entirely shared this view, and it was quickly agreed over the next few weeks that I should take one year of paid 'research leave' from 1 October 2000 and that an acting head would be appointed for the period of my absence.

I was due one term's research leave anyway and that facilitated this arrangement. In addition, I would have been entitled to up to six months' paid sick leave under the terms of my appointment, and I was clearly becoming increasingly unfit to work. Even so, it was a generous package. Both Michael and I hoped that I would be able to do a fair amount of research during this year, but at that stage we had no idea that my trial would be so delayed and it was the overriding intention that I would serve any term of imprisonment that might be imposed during this period of leave. As far as I know, only four people within college management, including the then Provost, were aware that I was being prosecuted for a motoring offence.

I saw Michael every month or two during the long wait for trial. We don't have much in common, so these meetings were pretty heavy going for both of us. Our meetings naturally enabled college to keep track of what was happening in my case, but I dare say that he was sincere in his repeated insistence that college was trying to be 'a good employer'.

What Michael did not appreciate was the publicity my case was likely to attract. He seemed convinced that it would not be reported in the national press. I was more doubtful as I was following newspaper reports on driving offences and could see that they attracted a fair amount of coverage. It would all depend on whether the newspapers had anything more interesting to print on the day, and I accepted that my trial just might pass unreported, especially if I were acquitted.

It was only much later that I learnt how important the presumption of non-publicity had been to college, but it was a great burden off my mind to feel that my job was safe during those long months of waiting for trial.

***

I had another and stronger reason for wanting to hang on to my job than all the obvious ones. For thirty-five years, history had been my ruling passion, and it was only by keeping my job that I could be sure of remaining a professional historian. I was resolved not to lose history and obsessed with continuing to undertake historical research.

This obsession shaded into another. The purpose of

prison is to take a part of your life away from you and to waste your time while you're behind bars. I was determined to beat the system if I were imprisoned by putting my time in jail to good use. That meant keeping on with historical research while I was inside and devising other useful ways of spending my time.

All this came together in the survival plan for life in prison which I wrote in the autumn of 2000 at Joe's prompting. History received the top priority. I drew up a list of about twenty hefty and difficult history books I ought to read and absorb so that Jannie could send them to me in prison by ones or twos, and placed them in a neat row on my bookshelves. I also decided that I would learn a new language in prison. At first, my thoughts turned to Italian, but I soon chose Latin and Ancient Greek – lots of word endings to memorise and go over in my head during long and perhaps sleepless nights. And I would keep a prison diary so that I could write about my experiences after my release. If forced to take on a 'job' in prison, I would regard it as slave labour and yet another attempt to waste my time. I would therefore drag my feet and do as little as I could without making myself liable to disciplinary proceedings. In all other respects, I would be a model prisoner, while making it clear to the other inmates that I was one of them and would never act as an informer. In short, I would give an outward impression of submission while withdrawing into an inner world and refusing to accept that prison had to function as a dark, wasteful hole.

**

My love of history helped to sustain me through much of the time when I was waiting for trial. It was one of the foremost psychological blocking mechanisms in my armoury. Reading and thinking about the motoring laws took up a lot of mental energy in the last months of 2000, but I was kept going above all through that bleak winter by writing a scholarly article for a historical journal. The article was long (17,000 words) and complicated. It demanded a lot of concentration from me. It has since been published.

I finished the article in April 2001, and it seemed pointless to start on any new piece of historical work before my trial. So how was I going to pass the time? For decades, I had dreamt about writing a novel, and now I finally did so. I wrote it in a frenzy of activity – eight or ten hours a day, 80,000 words in just over two months. That, as scholars of the old school (and novelists too, no doubt) would say, was probably 70,000 too many.

I chose to make it a whodunnit in a university setting. I didn't have much time, and the whodunnit genre gave me a structure and academic life provided a setting which required no research. The printout has lain in a drawer since July 2001, but I hope to publish it in a revised form one day. Whether or not the novel is ever published, it served me well – it kept my mind off the terrors of prison for over two months.

My final blocking mechanism was classical languages. They were in my survival plan for prison, but I saw no harm in obtaining a bit of foundation knowledge in advance. I had been looking at the basics of both Latin and Ancient Greek through the winter and spring in a sporadic sort of way, but I needed something more once my novel was written. I had three or four weeks left to my trial and I registered for an intensive eight-day beginner's course in Ancient Greek in mid-July 2001. I attended with punctilious regularity and enjoyed it tremendously. The course ended five days before my trial began.

All in all, I look back on those six and a half months as a good time. I felt so much better once the decision to plead not guilty was taken, and I had filled a period which the legal system is designed to turn into a living hell with activities that had been absorbing and useful. But I did not pass these months in any spirit of artificial optimism. My rage had given way to a grim fatalism. In December 2000 I had decided to roll the dice, and I would stand the hazard of the die. I left for Derby on the afternoon of Sunday, 22 July 2001 without much hope that I would be coming back in the near future.

II ROLLING THE DICE

Chapter Six
Derby (23-24 July 2001)

After all the waiting, I had expected my trial to involve a little more by way of drama. Instead, the proceedings were low key and subdued. The trial began at 10.30 in the morning and the judge concluded his summing up at around three in the afternoon. What prolonged the trial was that the jury did not return with a verdict for about twenty-four hours.

Derby Crown Court is a modern, functionalist kind of building set back from a busy road on the outskirts of the city centre. My trial was held on the second, top floor of the courthouse. There was a large concourse area and three or four courtrooms. The courtroom itself reminded me of a small lecture theatre in one of the new, concrete-slab universities erected in the Sixties. You entered through the public gallery – half a dozen or so rows of seats taking up one side of the room and facing the area occupied by the jury. The dock was to the right of the gallery and I sat there, along with a uniformed court officer, shielded by a presumably bullet-proof glass screen and facing the judge. The lawyers and the witness box were located in a slightly sunken bull-ring at the centre of the room. The paint was fresh, the carpet new and clean, but it was still a bleak and windowless place. It made me think of the sort of bunker where the terrified remnants of mankind might seek refuge in the aftermath of a nuclear or biochemical holocaust.

In front of the public gallery, there was a table for the press with two or three journalists behind it. One seemed senior to the others, a young man in a truly hideous short-sleeved check shirt. This could only be the local press, acting as stringers for the national dailies. The absence of a large press contingent was good. Less good was the presence of twelve or fifteen people in the public gallery whom I assumed to be the bereaved. I could not see them very clearly from the dock, but they were facing the jury, whose members would witness their reactions as the evidence was given. Annette and Alan were not happy about this, but it was inherent in the lay-out of the courtroom.

Before the jury was brought in, I entered a plea of not guilty to causing death by dangerous driving but guilty to careless driving. This was not a serious attempt at plea bargaining. We realised the CPS thought it could nail me and would not play ball. The prosecuting barrister duly refused this offer, and Judge Granville Shyler then said that it was up to defence to decide whether or not the jury should be informed that I was prepared to plead guilty to careless driving.

This was a tactical question, and I had spent a fair amount of time discussing it with Annette and Alan before we reached the courtroom. At the end of the trial, the jury would have the option of acquitting me of dangerous driving but finding me guilty of careless driving. Was it to my advantage to let the jury know that I had offered a plea of guilty to careless driving and that the offer had been rejected by the prosecution? On the principle that most people if faced with three choices (in this case guilty of dangerous driving, guilty of careless driving or not guilty of anything) will gravitate towards the compromise in the middle, it might have been damaging to eliminate from the outset the third and most lenient possibility. That was an argument for letting the jury hear a simple plea of not guilty *tout court*. On the other hand, to offer a plea of guilty to careless driving meant that I was acknowledging my responsibility for the accident and would avoid giving the impression that I expected to escape without any penalty at all. This approach seemed the wiser one. We had therefore agreed that the jury would be told of my spurned offer of guilty to careless driving, and they were.

My recollections of the court proceedings have a hazy, dreamlike quality. I found that my mind was constantly wandering. I was thinking about the case, but in a random way and not concentrating closely on what was being said at any particular moment. There was only one witness for the prosecution, a policeman from Chesterfield. He showed the timed version of the video supplied by the defence and described the various tyre marks that had been found on the surface of the motorway with the help of a large chart. After that, the statement I had made to the police at Chesterfield was read out with the policeman playing the role of PC Martin and the prosecuting barrister giving my words. Annette did not cross examine him, and that was it – the prosecution case was over.

We could not have been going for much more than an hour, when Annette stood up and called me as the only witness for the defence. I had been expecting her to make an opening address to the jury and didn't register for a few moments that I was being called. Annette's examination was very brief. She merely asked me to describe the accident as I had experienced it and took me through its psychological impact on me.

So far, so good, but now came the moment I had

feared for over a year: cross-examination. Annette had tried to reassure me that cross-examination is not as bad as it is presented in films and on TV. I also knew that I had told the truth, so there was in principle no need to be afraid. But I still was. Barristers are trained to make a witness look like an arsehole or a liar, and preferably both, during cross-examination. Jannie had repeatedly warned me that I tend to sound arrogant when I feel threatened. So I was both shit scared and doing my best to remain in humble mode when the prosecutor rose to his feet.

In the event, Annette proved to be right and cross-examination was not a fearsome ordeal. The prosecutor made the assumption that, as a Londoner, I had mainly used my car in the metropolis itself and asked me a series of questions designed to suggest that I had little experience of driving on *British* motorways. He seemed to accept what I said about long driving holidays on the continent, but dismissed the motorways there as nothing when compared to the rigours of the M1. He had obviously never been to Germany. I answered a trifle limply that I had used the M25 when going on these continental holidays.

Not that it mattered. This was trivial stuff. It was merely a curtain-raiser for the accusation he really wanted to put to me. This was that I was lying when I said that I had reached for my jacket in order to pull it onto my lap. What I had really been doing, he claimed, was trying to fish the mints out of the jacket pocket. He put the allegation to me in a normal voice, I denied it in an equally normal voice and then he just sat down. I'm not sure that the point has any real importance. Would fumbling in the pocket have been more negligent than reaching for the jacket? Perhaps the goal was merely to sow some seeds of doubt about my good character by putting it in the jury's mind that I might not be as truthful as I seemed. The whole cross-examination can't have taken more than somewhere between five and ten minutes.

Both Alan and Annette were not very happy with my performance in the witness box, and I too thought that I had not done very well. I felt I had been laconic and guarded. In particular, I was annoyed that in my nervousness I had forgotten to mention during cross-examination that my experience of British motorways was not limited to a few sorties onto the M25 and that in the two years before the accident I had used the M3 from London to Portsmouth quite often and twice driven halfway up the M1 itself and back.

It was still well before the lunch break, so there was time for closing speeches from both the prosecution and the defence. I didn't concentrate on either speech very well, but I was struck that both barristers kept saying that interpretation of the law was for the judge rather than them. As they both also agreed that the facts were not really in dispute, that didn't leave them much to talk about in theory. The prosecutor retreated into asserting that my driving was dangerous rather than careless – 'we say this was dangerous driving'. Annette was more bold and dipped her toe into interpreting the law by listing clear-cut examples of dangerous driving and contrasting them with the much lower degree of negligence I had displayed. She laid stress, naturally, on the fact that the period of my distraction from the road ahead had only been 1.96 seconds. But her final appeal was visceral – this could be you in the dock.

It was now past midday and the judge said he would deliver his summing-up after the lunch break. I had Jannie, my eldest son David and Sally, a loyal friend, with me in Derby, and the four of us went off for lunch in a tatty pub close to the courthouse. When we came back to the crown court, I noticed the young journalist with the alarming shirt sitting on a low brick wall out-side. On the other side of the path opposite him was a tallish tree. The trunk was quite thick, but not thick enough. As we waited for the traffic lights to change so that we could cross the road to the courthouse, I noticed a camera lens protruding from one side of the tree and the grubby trousers of a man's backside from the other.

The ambush was not very competently laid, but it did not need to be. There was no other route to follow and when we crossed the road, the check shirt signalled to the aspiring paparazzo, who emerged from behind the tree and took several photos of me as we walked past.

The court session resumed at two and Judge Shyler gave his summing-up. Once again, I found it difficult to concentrate, but it struck me as fair and balanced. He dwelt, of course, on the supreme tragedy of the proceedings, that three innocent people had died, but there was also a lot there that was pleasing to the defence. He accepted that I was 'traumatised' (his word) by the accident and its consequences and said that my previous good character entitled me to be believed. He gave me credit for giving evidence, stressing that I had been under no obligation to do so.

After the summing-up, the jury filed out and so did those involved in my case – while the jury deliberated, another hearing began in front of Judge Shyler. Court time is expensive and precious. The jury had with them both a transcript of my statement at Chesterfield Police Station and a timed copy of the video. About ninety minutes later, the court day was drawing to a close, and my case resumed so that the jury could be asked if it had reached a verdict. The answer was 'no', and proceedings were adjourned until the following morning. I was given unconditional bail for the night, and we had to book ourselves back into the guest-house where we had stayed the previous night.

The situation was quite unexpected – I had imagined that I would either be in prison or on my way back to London by the close of business on Monday. Instead, I was suspended in limbo. But I remember that Monday night in Derby as a cheerful occasion, almost a happy one. We were all in high spirits, though it's hard to see why. I suppose it was that we were still in with a chance.

My trial resumed the next morning, but by lunchtime the jury still didn't have a verdict. I spent the time in the concourse area outside the courtroom. They were long hours of desultory chatting and heavy smoking, but not of acute anxiety. The situation seemed unreal, dream-like, and I awaited the verdict with fatalism and resignation.

After lunch the judge told the jury that he would accept a majority verdict, and that broke the logjam. The jury was back within an hour or so. I was hanging around the concourse area as usual when Annette came hurrying up to me, pulling on her wig, and said 'The jury's back !' This is the supreme moment of drama in any contested trial, and there was complete silence as we waited to hear the verdict. I noted that not a single juror looked at me as they came in and felt certain that the verdict would be 'guilty'. And 'guilty' it was, by a majority of eleven to one. The bereaved families in the public gallery behaved with dignity and decorum. There were no cheers or jeers, just the same silence.

I had learnt thirty minutes earlier from Annette that the judge had indicated that he was prepared to have pre-sentencing reports prepared rather than proceed to immediate sentencing in the event of a guilty verdict. This was an unexpected development as Annette had always assumed until then that I would be sent to prison on the day if I lost. Now there would be a few weeks for a probation officer to interview me and write a report on my remorse, the likelihood of my reoffending and the effect that various sentences might have on me and my family.

This was good news in that it suggested that the judge was not thinking in terms of a draconian or exemplary sentence. When I asked Annette if it meant that eighteen months was now more likely than two years, she replied, 'Yes – or less.'

When the jury had been discharged, Annette duly asked for pre-sentencing reports; Judge Shyler agreed and granted me continuing unconditional bail until I returned to court for sentencing. But he added that, since there had been three deaths, a custodial sentence was 'almost inevitable', and he asked me whether I understood that. I replied from the dock, 'Yes, I understand,' and the trial was over.

Afterwards, I spoke with Annette and Alan in a tiny 'conference room' next to the courtroom for about thirty minutes. We did this partly to give the bereaved families time to leave the courthouse before I came out. We hoped, but did not really believe, that the press might go away too. Our conference was a gloomy occasion, but Annette was sure that we had been right to take the case to trial, even though we had lost. She thought that my previous good character and clean driving record, the frank nature of my statement to the police and above all the point about the 1.96 seconds had been rammed home in a way that would not have been possible if I had pleaded guilty. Annette was much heartened by the judge's willingness to defer sentencing, but she was not optimistic that I would escape prison and added that she thought the prosecution would appeal against sentence if I did.

On that low note, we set off for Derby station. Our party split up. David and Sally went back to the guesthouse to collect our luggage, while I rode in a taxi direct to the station with Jannie, Annette and Alan. The courthouse was becoming deserted as we descended to the ground floor, but we could see two or three photographers loitering outside. This prompted more conferring over how to avoid letting them get a shot of me, but I eventually decided that, as I was neither a paedophile nor a drug dealer, I'd be damned if I was going to walk out of the court with a bag over my head. So Alan went out first and found a taxi and the photographers got their snaps of me as I walked past them.

On the train back to London, we were a strangely jolly party. I felt unaccountably cheerful for a man who was almost certainly headed for prison. It was mainly relief that the tension of waiting was over and that I was getting the hell out of Derby on a mercifully rapid train. Relief also that I had a few weeks of freedom left – an evil deferred always feels at the time like an evil avoided. And there was still the chance, however slim, that I might not go to prison, even though I did not really dare to hope that I would get a suspended sentence.

I also felt vindicated in my view of the motoring laws and in my decision to plead not guilty. I do not know what went on within the jury, but I find it difficult to believe that one man or woman could have held out alone against eleven other jurors for twenty-four hours. It seems more probable that there must have been at least one or two more who were initially on my side, but who were gradually worn down by, and subsumed within, the majority. The behaviour of the jury lent support to my belief that the distinction between dangerous and careless driving is not clear-cut or easy to define.

That gave me some comfort. So did more primitive instincts. I had not given the prosecution my head on a plate, and the jury had not been back in five minutes with a guilty verdict. I had forced the prosecution to fight for the conviction and it had not been a quick or easy victory for them. All of this did something to alleviate the horror of my defeat.

On a more pragmatic level, it also seemed that the judge had not been deeply alienated by my not-guilty plea. Perhaps the penalty for it in terms of sentence would not be all that severe? I didn't know it at the time, but Annette was to be proved right that I had gained rather than lost by taking the case to trial. Just how much I had gained would become clear over the next few weeks.

Chapter Seven
The glare of publicity

It was late in the evening before Jannie and I arrived home on the day of my conviction, so we never knew what was reported on radio and TV about my case. But it clearly received a fair amount of prominence on the news as there were already three or four messages on our answering service from friends who had been unaware that I was being prosecuted.

Publicity was no surprise – the photographers lurking outside Derby Crown Court had already suggested that there would be some. My case was reported in most national newspapers the next day – Wednesday, 25 June – often in some detail, though not always with complete accuracy. Because of my Danish surname, my case even made it into one of the Danish tabloids. For natural reasons, I had been following motoring cases in the press for the previous fifteen months, and I knew the way 'killer drivers' had frequently been presented. I expected to be vilified and traduced.

In the event, I was relieved by the press coverage. Most of it was factual and neutral in tone. There was no character assassination and little suggestion of gloating that my imprisonment was virtually certain. Nearly all the papers reported what Annette and I had said about my remorse in court and my resolution never to drive again. Above all, they homed in on the point that my distraction had been limited to 1.96 seconds.

The nature of the press coverage was a weight off my mind. My despondency was also alleviated by the telephone calls and letters expressing sympathy and support that I began to receive. Some were from old friends, but others were from individuals I knew very slightly through my work and a few from people whom I did not regard as particularly well disposed towards me. I was very heartened.

Even so, I went in to University College at the end of the week in an apprehensive mood. Would I be shunned? Would people gaze surreptitiously at me out of the corners of their eyes? In short, would I be some sort of leper or freak? The reality was far better than my fears. It was the height of the summer vacation, so college was quiet with almost no students and few academics about, but I was greeted everywhere either in the normal way as if nothing had happened or by 'if there's anything I can do' style statements. Only one person deliberately ignored me.

Rank-and-file members of college could offer moral support, but I also needed to clarify my position with college management. I saw Michael Worton on 27 June, the Friday after my trial. It quickly struck me that college management seemed to be considering my predicament for the first time. Many matters that I thought settled now appeared to be the subject of emergency discussions at senior level. At some points in my conversation with Michael, it almost seemed as if all our meetings over the previous fourteen months had never taken place. This lent a touch of the surreal to the conversation, at least for me. I gained the strong impression that what had thrown everything into the melting pot was the publicity attracted by my trial.

The most worrying point in the interview came when Michael looked at me earnestly and said that college would, 'I'm afraid', have to take legal advice about my case. I had rather thought that college had done that fourteen months earlier. The whole premise of our conversation until then had appeared to be that I would return to work after my release from prison, but Michael now seemed to be giving me a veiled warning that there might be moves to dismiss me from my post. The warning was oblique, but in an institution where so many agendas lie concealed one beneath the other, it could almost be counted as positively direct.

We didn't shake hands when I left Michael's office and we have never spoken or communicated since. I came away unsure as to where I now stood with college. My future position seemed shrouded with confusion and uncertainty. It still sounded on balance as if there would be no attempt to sack me, but how could I be sure of anything when college policy towards me seemed fluid and to be evolving on a day-to-day basis? There was nothing I could do about it beyond giving my union a detailed written account with supporting documentation of my dealings with college in case the union had to represent me while I was in prison. I also sorted the books and papers in my office so that Jannie and David could clear it of my personal belongings if the worst came to the worst.

My conversation with Michael also brought into focus a question I had been mulling over for some months – my position as head of department. I had gradually been moving to the conclusion that, even if I escaped imprisonment, I was too traumatised by everything that had happened since the accident to cope in the immediate future with the stress that came with the headship. At all events, that's the reason I gave for my resignation as head of department in the letter I sent to the Provost.

**

Apart from talking to my employers and my union, I had a lot of other things to deal with during these three weeks of 'pre-sentencing'. I spoke sometimes to Alan on the phone, but there was no meeting with my lawyers about what would be said in mitigation. The protocol seemed to be that this was a matter for Annette's discretion.

About a week after my trial, I received through Alan a copy of a letter that Valerie Kempton, the mother of the younger man killed in the accident, had addressed to the judge. It was also signed by her surviving son and her daughter-in-law, and its contents were remarkable. The letter stated that they believed my imprisonment would 'serve no purpose at all' and that 'enough lives have been lost and broken without adding to the total'. They therefore asked the court to deal 'fairly and compassionately' with me. Valerie Kempton had been quoted in the press the day after my conviction as saying that she did not want to see me sent to jail, but that was quite different from a formal, reasoned letter to the court. The letter could only be, and was meant to be, very helpful to my chances of staying out of prison, and I was tremendously moved by it. So was Jannie. I was astonished that the Kempton family could overcome their grief to that extent and display such a clear perception of the limitations of vengeance. I replied to them, through the court, thanking them for their 'humanity and compassion'.

My hopes were also raised when I rang Jackie Smith (not her real name), the probation officer dealing with my case, to make an appointment so that she could prepare her pre-sentencing report. She spoke as if a suspended sentence might be a real possibility, and she remained upbeat on this point when I saw her on 2 August. She told me that offences like mine came into the tiny category of unintentional crime. They were also 'very emotive' and produced highly divergent reactions: some people thought that someone like me should not go to jail at all, while others believed that the sentences for 'killer drivers' were far too short. In fact, my case had created some debate in the probation office, and the officer originally assigned to it had said that he/she 'couldn't deal with it'. Finally, Jackie had said that she would take my file. Jackie volunteered the information that she could not honestly say that she had never momentarily taken her eyes off the road or a hand off the wheel while driving.

So what is a pre-sentencing report? It is intended for

the eyes of the judge, and I didn't get a copy of mine until thirty minutes before I was due to go into court for sentencing. I've still got it, and I can see that such reports follow a standard pattern. They describe the crime (the 'offence analysis') and the criminal (the 'offender assessment') and then go on to consider how much of a risk to the public is posed by the criminal and the likelihood of reoffending. They also discuss the degree of remorse shown by the offender and the psychological and financial effects of imprisonment on him and his family. They conclude with some tentative suggestions about which sentences might be appropriate.

I got some idea of what ground the report would cover from my conversation with Jackie. I was struck by the way I had to produce bank and other statements to prove what I said about financial commitments and to show Jackie the sleeping pills I was on. This enabled her to write 'verified' after some of the comments in her report. Probation officers doubtless hear a lot of tall stories in circumstances like these. Jackie was clearly sympathetic to me, but she wasn't a soft touch and questioned me quite closely on some points.

Jackie said she would go as close to recommending a suspended sentence as convention allows (judges apparently don't like any hint of being told what to do), and she was true to her word. When I later saw her report, it concluded by suggesting that 'the Court may feel able to consider the merits of suspending any period of custody imposed'. The report also contained the observation that 'this tragic offence was the result of ... a momentary lapse of concentration rather than a deliberate attempt to flout the law with a premeditated act of dangerous driving'. I found that a rather neat definition of a distinction that I have been trying to make throughout this book.

***

It was also during these weeks that the first approaches from the press for an interview reached me. All of them promised that the interview would be 'sympathetic' and conducted by a highly 'sensitive' reporter. Not for me some dandruff-encrusted Lunchtime O'Booze – full of sordid bonhomie, but short on empathy.

I was very wary. The press coverage of my trial had not been hostile in the way I had feared, but – like most people – I distrusted the newspapers. Perhaps they would promise 'sympathetic' treatment and then do a hatchet job. On the other hand, any chance of secrecy was gone and my case was now in the public domain. An interview would give me an opportunity to express my views about the motoring laws and sentencing policy.

Here was a chance for someone other than the road safety lobby, which is frequently clamouring for more and longer prison sentences, to make his voice heard. In this case, the class system was working to my advantage. The press assumed that, as a university teacher, I would be reasonably articulate and coherent. Convicted motorists don't often get asked for interviews, I suspect.

In the end, I agreed to give an interview for the review section of the *Times*, provided it was embargoed until after sentencing. The interview took place in my office at college late on the afternoon of Friday, 10 August. It was conducted by Carol Midgley and lasted ninety minutes or so. I liked Carol and we spoke more easily and naturally than I expected. The betrayal I feared did not take place. The article that was published did prove to be sympathetic – in fact, it could not realistically have been more sympathetic – and it accounts for most, perhaps all, of the letters from strangers that I received while I was in prison. I had anticipated less human-interest material and more on the law, but Carol probably showed better judgement than me in telling it mainly as a human story seen from my perspective – and the legal points I wanted to make were included, at least in outline.

After my interview for the *Times* there was a last weekend before sentencing. I remember it as warm and pleasant, a happy couple of days. Despite the letter from the Kempton family and Jackie's recommendation of a suspended sentence, I did not allow myself to hope that I would escape prison. But I was determined to survive and that determination was permeated by defiance. In those days, the words of Lucifer in *Paradise Lost* kept recurring in my mind.

> All is not lost; th'unconquerable will,
> And study of revenge, immortal hate,
> And courage never to submit or yield:
> And what is else not to be overcome.

I quoted the last two lines sometimes when replying to some of the supportive letters that had reached me. Tact made me omit the first two, but they spoke just as powerfully to me as the third and fourth. I faced prison with terror in my heart, but also full of unspoken hatred and defiance towards the legal system that was putting me there. I'm still proud of that defiance, less so of the hatred.

Chapter Eight
Stoke on Trent (14 August 2001)

Judge Shyler was sitting at Stoke Crown Court, not Derby, on 14 August, and that is where I was sentenced. My case was set for 10.30 in the morning on a Tuesday, so the same gang of four – Jannie, David, Sally and me – travelled to Stoke the previous afternoon. We went out for a meal and a drink afterwards, but the atmosphere was very different from what it had been in Derby while awaiting the verdict three weeks earlier. We were all tense and gloomy and made an early night of it.

In the morning, I gave my ID and bank cards to Jannie so that there was nothing in my wallet except for the fifty pounds in cash I would take with me to prison. I also emptied my briefcase of everything other than the items I hoped the prison authorities would allow me to keep – three books, envelopes and writing paper, some files with documents relating to my case and my employment.

When we arrived at Stoke Crown Court, there were only one or two journalists and one photographer waiting outside. The photographer filmed Jannie and me entering the court, the journalists followed me in. The courthouse was fairly deserted compared with Derby, but built in the same functionalist style.

There was a brief conference with Annette while I read the pre-sentencing report. And then we were in court for sentencing. The courtroom seemed very empty compared with the trial. Two or three journalists, no jury, of course, but also no policemen.

The prosecuting barrister did not wish to say anything, so Annette started out on her speech in mitigation at once. As during my trial, I found it difficult to concentrate and I do not recall much of what she said. She began by stressing that we had not wasted court time by calling a lot of witnesses etc. and by expressing the hope that I would not therefore be penalised for my not-guilty plea.

At this point, Judge Shyler interrupted her and said that there would be no such penalty. My conduct during the trial, he said, had been 'dignified and exemplary', and it had been 'perfectly reasonable' to put the question of whether my driving had been dangerous or careless to a jury. I could hardly believe my ears. After everything I had heard about the 'discount' given for a guilty plea, the judge was brushing the point aside on the grounds that my guilt had not been self-evident. I was so taken aback that my memory of the rest of Annette's address is very hazy, except that it did not last for more than another five minutes or so.

After that came the fearful moment – the sentence. Judge Shyler began by saying that he did not 'require' me to stand to hear it. I had been steeling myself to 'look impassive', as the newspapers put it, and that was a lot easier sitting down behind my bullet-proof glass. Once again, I cannot remember much of what the judge said. I was too focused on waiting for the bottom line. But I do recall that he read out the letter from the Kempton family, which he described as 'courageous', and that he referred to the 'exceptional circumstances' of the case. I was almost daring to hope that I might get a non-custodial sentence, when he pronounced the fateful word 'however'. The fact remained that three people had died and he was therefore sentencing me to ninety days in prison. He also banned me from driving for three years.

According to the newspaper clippings Jannie and David collected the next day, Judge Shyler observed that the case was 'a lesson to us all, how a moment's inattention can lead to disaster'. Apparently, he said that he had no option but to jail me despite the letter from the Kempton family and despite my 'character, reputation and remorse'. The judge also told me that my sentence would have been longer but for the letter from the Kempton family. I have no recollection of any of this, but that's what the papers say.

The pronouncement of sentence was followed by the classic formula, 'Take him down.' I just had time to exchange a quick glance with Jannie and David before the court officer with me in the dock opened a door by its side, stepped through it and with a sweeping gesture of his arm indicated that I should follow. They clearly only drag you from the dock when they have to. I did so, and the officer handcuffed my wrist to his with the apology, 'I'm sorry but I have to do this.'

We went down several flights of stairs into the bowels of the courthouse. I was searched and lost my tie and braces. I was allowed to keep my shoelaces – in contrast to some of the poor bastards I would see in prison shambling about in floppy, unlaced shoes.

My first couple of hours in custody were a kind of intermediate stage between liberty and the full rigours of incarceration. The uniformed court officers, who are neither policemen nor prison officers, were extremely kind both to me and to my family. Jannie and David were allowed to visit me, though we were separated by a glass screen and had to speak through microphones. It was a difficult leave-taking, but we were all tremendously relieved that my sentence was so much shorter than we had anticipated.

Annette was also pleased at the outcome, and ventured the guess that the prosecution would probably not appeal against my sentence. She suggested that I release a statement to the media simply saying that our thoughts were with the bereaved families. This is a standard formula in the circumstances, I suspect. It did not strike me as quite right. I thought the pretence of being unconcerned at my own imprisonment would seem insincere and I also felt that a word of thanks to the Kempton family was appropriate. The statement which I wrote and which Annette read out to the media outside the courthouse was therefore a little longer than she had suggested. It ran:

> Nothing that has happened to myself or my family can compare to the tragedy that struck those who died in the accident and the suffering of their families. I am deeply grateful for the humanity and compassion shown to me by the Kempton family. I sincerely hope that everyone touched by this tragedy can begin to find peace now that the trial is over.

That was an honest statement of how I felt, but the last sentence was probably over-optimistic. It certainly has been for me.

Some time around three o'clock, I think, the message came through that the vehicle which would take me to prison had arrived in the basement of the courthouse. It was time to go.

***

But before I go, a final word about the law. So what lessons can be deduced from my trial and sentencing? First of all, I believe that my views on our motoring laws and sentencing policy were vindicated. Judge Shyler's observation that it had been 'perfectly reasonable' to put the question of whether my driving had been dangerous or careless to a jury and the fact that one juror at least held out for me for twenty-four hours support my arguments that the distinction between the two most serious forms of negligent driving is insufficiently clear-cut.

It is also pretty clear from what the judge said when sentencing me that I was only sent to prison because of the gravity of the consequences of my error, not the nature of the error itself. The sentence was lenient, merciful even, given how long it might have been, and to that extent I have to acknowledge that the legal system proved more flexible than anyone, including my lawyers, had thought possible. Some crude tariff of x number of months or years per death had not been applied. That makes me think somewhat better of our judges and our legal system, but does not change my view that the existence of 'causing death by dangerous driving' as an offence is morally and intellectually indefensible.

All the legal proceedings were overshadowed by one supreme irony – that I gained rather than lost by pleading not guilty, even though I was convicted. The terrifying discount factor never came into play. If there had not been a contested trial, if I had not given evidence, neither the judge nor the Kempton family would have had an opportunity to hear an account of the accident from my own lips or to form a direct impression of my personality. I cannot say what effect that had on them, but it may be that the Kempton family would not have written their letter to the judge without it. There certainly would not have been a three-week gap for pre-sentencing reports, so there would not have been time for them to write before I was sentenced.

The day was rounded off with another delicious irony. When Jannie arrived home from Stoke, she found a letter waiting for me. It contained the inconvenience we all dread – a summons to perform jury service, the first ever sent to me. Jannie rang the court to explain the circumstances, and some days later a new letter hit the doormat from the 'Jury Summoning Officer'. It stated: 'As you are not qualified for jury service, I have withdrawn the summons. You need not attend court, or take any further action.' I hope the disqualification stands for life. Having been on the receiving end of a jury verdict, I would hate to hold anyone else's fate in my hands.

During those hours I spent in the depths of Stoke Crown Court, I was tremendously relieved at my sentence. Ninety days. That meant I would be automatically released after forty-five. Just over six weeks! And, because the sentence was less than twelve months, I would not have to report to a probation officer for a period after my release (indeed I would not have a probation officer at all) and there would be no restrictions on my movements – I could go abroad the day I got out if I wanted. It also seemed inconceivable that I could be dismissed from my job for 'non-performance of duties' over such a short period.

All good stuff, but the other side of the coin was that, even so, I was about to spend forty-five days within the coils of the British prison system, that strange foreign country from which travellers return but rarely bring tales. I would be on my own in a terrifying and unfamiliar environment. I was shit scared.

III Cat B

Chapter Nine
Arrival at Shrewsbury jail

The senior court officer at Stoke Crown Court, a kindly old gentleman who tried to prepare me for what was coming, told me that what had happened to me would 'begin to sink in' once I was in the van headed for prison. He was dead right.

I was taken down, handcuffed to a court officer, from the detention area in the courthouse to a closed van in the basement. The official name for these vans is 'cellular vehicle', but everyone in the system calls them 'sweat boxes'. Behind each of the van's square windows was an individual cage with a plastic seat and a door that is both locked and chained. I was led into one such cage and the cuffs were only removed when the door was almost closed, my cuffed right hand sticking awkwardly out through the opening. There must be about ten cages on both sides of the central aisle in each sweat box.

I think I was the only prisoner in the vehicle when we left the court, but as we drove, we picked up more people sentenced to prison from at least two magistrates courts. They sounded young and they were raucous at first. I could hear them swearing and complaining that smoking was not allowed in the van and calling out to each other, 'How long did you get?' Three or four months seemed the going rate that day.

It took about an hour to drive to Shrewsbury prison. The shouting from the other prisoners gradually abated and the only sound was the radio, which played pop music interspersed with short news bulletins. I heard a brief report about my own case on one such bulletin. The cage was small with too little room for one's feet, the plastic seat made my bum ache and it was quite hot. It was an uncomfortable journey and now, cut off from my family and lawyers, I felt isolated and apprehensive about what was to come. I remember that drive as one of the lowest moments of my imprisonment. In all respects, the sweat box lived up to its name.

It was hard to see much of the prison from the sweat box, but I have an impression of a narrow driveway passing through two sets of huge and seemingly impregnable gates. Abandon all hope, you who enter here! We drove for a short way beyond the gates and all I can remember is high walls topped with barbed wire. The sweat box halted outside what in prisons is called 'reception', the set of rooms through which inmates pass when entering or leaving.

About ten of us were let out of the van and told to go into two waiting rooms – one for new arrivals and the other for remand prisoners who had only been let out for the day to attend court. A second sweat box arrived a little later bringing more prisoners.

The waiting room was a filthy, sordid place. There was an unflushed toilet partially concealed behind a low partition, a table, a hard bench and a few plastic chairs. We were given cheese sandwiches and a cup of tea, since we were too late for the prison dinner. This was the moment I had feared – my first encounter with other prisoners and with the screws. I'll call prison officers 'screws' most of the time, by the way, without meaning any particular offence. The term was universally employed inside and it's hard to shake off. I'll also use the words 'prisoner' and 'inmate' interchangeably. I was told that old-school, hard-line screws don't like 'inmate' as it confers too much dignity on the prisoners, but it was widely used, even by some prison officers.

The prisoners in the reception waiting room seemed very young, scruffy and dirty and – praise the Lord! – they didn't take much interest in me. They all spoke with strong Midland accents except me and one other man, a swarthy East European. He claimed to understand little English, but had picked up a few essentials. He explained that he was on remand charged with eight burglaries, 'but they've got no forensic'. The only other prisoner who spoke to me a fair bit was a short, skeletal and alarmingly cross-eyed young man with a shaven head and bad teeth. He was called 'Donnie' (from Donovan) and told me with a sly grin that he had been done for 'receiving stolen property'. His main interest in me seemed to lie in cadging cigarettes. He managed to extract two off me. I was still too frightened to refuse, but I learnt within a day or two just to say 'Fuck off'.

I was the last prisoner to pass through reception, and the governor turned up to talk to me as I was waiting alone. He was clearly familiar with my case and said that he would get me transferred as soon as possible to an open prison – probably Ford in West Sussex so that I would be close to my home and family. And he assured me that, although the first week in prison would seem very long, the remaining five would pass quickly. That didn't prove to be true, but it was kindly meant. He then accompanied me during the first phase of passing through reception. He didn't say anything, but I'm sure that it was thanks to him that I was allowed to keep all my papers and books.

I then had to strip behind a partition, but with an

officer watching (though I was given a towel to put round my waist). I folded my clothes into a box which the officers closed and stored. I then had a shower from a primitive head sticking from a wall at chest height, while a prisoner who worked in the store brought me clothes – red and grey tee shirts, two long-sleeved jogging tops, one pair of jeans (so tight I never wore them) and one pair of joggers, six pairs of underpants (some too small) and six pairs of socks. I was also given bedding and four medium-sized towels which all gave off the same unpleasant stink. The socks in prison are thick and coarse. As another prisoner said to me, the two things you really want in prison are your own underpants and your own socks.

The only clothing I could keep was my shoes – one of the two reception officers advised me to take advantage of this privilege, since 'prison shoes aren't very good'. I was also allowed to keep what was left in my packet of cigarettes. When I asked about matches, the other reception officer handed me his disposable lighter – a small but human gesture.

I was also given a plastic mug, toothpaste, toothbrush, comb and bar of soap along with a plastic dessert spoon, fork and knife (one of each). Dressed in my new prison clothes and carrying the rest of my things in a sack, I was taken through a great metal door into the prison proper. The whole process of waiting and passing through reception probably took about ninety minutes.

Prisoners are not allowed to have cash, and any money in your possession when you reach prison is taken off you. It constitutes what is called your 'private money' along with any funds sent on your behalf by family or friends. Prisoners are allowed to spend a certain portion of their private money every week (£10 is the norm, I think), along with their allowance from the prison (a fiver a week in Shrewsbury, if my memory serves me) on 'buying' permitted items once a week. Along with the other new arrivals, I was given a pack of tobacco, phonecards and chocolate bars on the morning after admission to the prison. The value of the pack was set against my first weekly allowance.

I did not see much of the prison interior that night, because I was put in one of the first cells past the great door, but it gave the impression of a huge aircraft hanger. The cell itself was filthy. Just outside my cell there was a sort of bungalow within the great dome of the hanger. It contained three or four rooms and was 'the landing office' – the administrative centre for the ground floor of the prison, the place where the screws hung out. I was taken there twice to see different senior screws and then again to see the prison doctor.

The risk of suicide is what topped the agenda and the associated question of whether I was more likely to do myself in if I spent the night alone in my cell. I was very keen to have some time to reflect on how I would get through the next forty-five days, so I vigorously denied suicidal intent. It was only after the prison doctor gave his approval that I was spared a cellmate for my first night in prison.

Back in my cell, I was visited by two prisoners with badges bearing the word 'Listener'. They had a box of paperbacks in case I wanted to read and told me that I could contact them any time, day or night, if I needed to talk by using the emergency buzzer in my cell. The Listeners were clearly another element in the suicide-prevention system of the prison. I didn't need or want to talk, but the two who came to see me seemed like very decent guys.

After they had gone, I switched on the TV and I was astonished to see footage of me and Jannie walking into Stoke Crown Court that morning as the lead item on ITV's *News at Ten*. It was an eerie sight and a sinister reminder of how the day had started in a hotel room in Stoke and ended in a filthy cell in Shrewsbury jail. The publicity seemed a matter of total insignificance. The reality of prison was all that counted. I was in shock, I suppose, but I had survived my first encounter with the prison system. Both screws and inmates had proved less menacing than I had feared. Just one night of sleep to round off the day, and forty-four more nights to get through.

Chapter Ten
Shrewsbury: 23-hour bang-up

In the end, I only stayed eight nights in Shrewsbury Prison, but it made a tremendous impression on me. The physical environment was dismal and intimidating. It resembled nothing so much as a dark, satanic mill. This is a Victorian prison built to instil terror and submission. The cells ran along the painted brick walls of one great warehouse of a room, and they were on four levels. There was a metal walkway along the cells on the three higher levels. Originally, that must have been it, but thick meshing with a canvas cover had since created mini-roofs above the ground and third floor levels.

The phone booths and the food serving area were on the ground floor, along with the main landing office, but each of the three upper floors had a smaller office. I was told by one screw that there was still a functional gallows somewhere in the prison – unused for forty or fifty years, but kept in trim in case capital punishment is reintroduced. Perhaps he was pulling my leg. Somewhere out there too was the wing for 'segregated' inmates – prisoners, mostly sex offenders but with a sprinkling of policemen and screws, isolated from the others at their own request. They had a routine and timetable of their own, and I never saw any of them.

'Exercise' – one hour a day in the open air – was taken in 'the cage', an area of asphalt just outside the main body of the cells. The cage was contained by a high wire fence and lay within the prison yard, which itself was enclosed by an even higher stone wall. There wasn't much room in the cage, and when a high proportion of the prisoners came out for exercise, it was very crowded. Inmates walked repeatedly in circles around the perimeter of the cage or sat against the fence chatting. Exercise was cancelled on at least two of the days that I was in Shrewsbury – I never found out why.

Eating was not a social event. You collected a metal tray from outside the food serving area. The tray was not intended for crockery. It had three depressions and your food was dispensed into them by prisoners wearing see-though plastic gloves. You never received plates or bowls, and you kept reusing the three pieces of plastic cutlery given to you when you were admitted to prison.

Once you'd got your food, you took the tray back to your cell to eat and were locked in. Half an hour later the door opened and you were told to place the tray on the floor by the cell door.

My cell had a bunk bed, a washbasin and a WC behind a low partition wall. If there were two to a cell (and that was the norm), you could neither wash nor shit in private. The same goes for having a shower. If you were 'offered' a shower (and it was a week before I was), you took it in a washroom beside the food serving area. There were low partition walls between each of the eight or so showers, but that's as far as privacy went. The rest of the time you had to do your best at the washbasin. Maybe this is why so many of the young men in Shrewsbury were perpetually digging into their joggers to scratch their genitals – itchy nuts caused by inadequate washing facilities.

In Shrewsbury, you shaved with a disposable razor available from the landing office in return for a used one. No kind of lather or aftershave were provided. There was no mirror in my cell. As Lee, the chief cleaner on my landing, pointed out, when prisoners were moved from the ground floor to higher landings, they often ripped the mirrors off the wall, fearing that there would be none in their new cell.

This was a pain, since it meant shaving and combing

my hair blind. I could feel the cuts and I often noticed during my first days in Shrewsbury that there were uneven patches of stubble here and there when I passed my hand over my face. I must have looked a right mess. Then I started borrowing Lee's mirror and matters improved. Lee kept his mirror well hidden in his cell and, like some of the screws, advised me always to slam my cell door behind when let out for exercise – as Lee put it, 'there's a lot of thieves in this place'.

The cell also had two chairs and tables and three storage units – two for the prisoners' belongings, the other as a base for the great luxury of the cell – the TV. I was told by one of the screws that there had only been a TV in every cell for a couple of weeks. There were no curtains or blinds on the window, which was blocked by both outer metal bars and an inner heavy wire mesh. There was not much room for pacing the floor, but I still did from time to time, prowling the cell like a caged tiger. Every item in the cell, particularly the washbasin and the WC, was filthy.

There were also two notice-boards above the top bunk. One had pictures of girls cut out from newspapers (some starkers, some fully clothed, most in between) and the paper was yellowing and cracked. The other was bare, but an inmate had engraved it with the legend:

Kevin Reilly

+

Lynidsey [sic] Scanlon

F-E [meaning 'forever', I suppose]

2001

The prison woke up at 7.30, when you heard a shout of 'Unlock!' outside and all the doors were opened. You then had till 8 a.m. to make 'applications' at the landing office. This was an important window of opportunity – mainly for pre-booking five-minute phone calls in the evening, but any request that involved the slightest divergence from routine seemed to require an 'application'.

Breakfast was at 7.50 and you were locked in (except for passing out the tray) until 'exercise' from eleven to twelve. Lunch was at noon, dinner at five, and you were locked in again after getting each meal. Apart from Wednesdays, when it was my landing's turn to have 'association' from six to eight, you were only unlocked to make a pre-booked phonecall after collecting your dinner. This is what's called 'twenty-three-hour bang up'.

During association, all the inmates on a particular landing were let out together so that they could 'associate' on the ground floor of the prison. Some prisoners did talk to each other, but just as many sat in front of a big-screen TV on the ground floor landing – an odd thing to do when watching TV was how they spent most of the time in their cells.

The only inmates to escape twenty-three-hour bang up were those who had 'work'. I got the impression from talking to other prisoners that few of them did work. The only ones you noticed were the prisoners who acted as kitchen assistants and cleaners. From my cell, I often heard music and shouting from the nearby workshop during the daytime, but it could easily have been a small number of men making a lot of noise.

I often found it sinister to hear the chatter of conversation among the cleaners outside my cell door and, once they were gone, the incessant rattle of the numerous keys carried on a chain by all screws. I had a sensation of bustling but inaccessible life outside. I could not investigate, of course, because the heavy iron door of the cell could only be opened from the outside. The screws could look into my cell by pulling back a flap that covered a spyhole in the cell door, but I could not look out. I could, however, peep through the gaps on each side of the door, and I often used to do this just for an imperfect glimpse of the world outside.

A few cells down from me was another man in his fifties who had a cell of his own. I never saw him very clearly, but his solitary monologues are still very vivid in my mind. He had bursts of shouting abuse at an imaginary person, threatening wounding and death in repetitive but lurid terms. He was particularly active in the evenings after dinner. Once he was in full flow when there was an equally loud shout from another cell – 'Shut up, nuthead!' That silenced him for five minutes, after which he started again. I learnt that he was called Smithie and had been in Shrewsbury prison before – in 1999. It was clear from conversation with a couple of the screws that they could see that he needed medical help not imprisonment. They seemed to respect him as quite an intelligent man when he was not having one of his spates of ranting.

**

The monotonous routine I've just described only kicked in with the weekend. The first three days involved a bit more out-of-cell activity – these were the days of 'induction' for new prisoners. The first and most essential part of induction is a series of brief interviews with prison officers to establish your 'security category'. There are four. The top two supposedly cover the real hard men. A and B are for prisoners whose escape must be 'impossible' or 'very difficult' respectively. Category C is for 'prisoners who cannot be trusted in open conditions, but who do not have the resources and will to make a determined escape attempt'. This must be the most humiliating classification – you want to escape but you're too lazy or thick to try it. Finally there is Category (or 'Cat' as it is called in prison jargon) D for 'prisoners who can reasonably be trusted in open conditions'.

The quotations come from the *Prisoners' Information Book*, and they may bear some relationship to how prisoners are classified in reality. Everyone, starting with my lawyers, had assumed that I would be a Cat D prisoner and that indeed was the classification given to me. I'm not sure, though, whether it had much to do with a serious assessment of whether I would try to escape. It seemed to me that virtually all inmates without previous convictions were made Cat D.

Classification is important because all the prisons in the country are divided into the same four categories. Being Cat D meant that I was eligible to serve my sentence in a Category D or 'open' prison. Anyone given a custodial sentence finds that his first port of call is the nearest 'local' prison, and like all local prisons, Shrewsbury was Cat B. Once you have been classified, you can be moved on to a prison corresponding to your category. But you do not have to be if you have a short sentence. I feared that I would not be moved for that reason, but in fact – as the governor had promised when I arrived – I was told within two or three days that I would be going to Ford open prison in West Sussex some time the following week.

That was lucky. I cannot say what I have to thank for this – the kindness of the prison authorities at Shrewsbury or the gross overcrowding in the prison or a combination of both. Donnie was less fortunate. He told me that he had been classified as Cat A and that he was really pissed off about it. I suspect he had a lot of 'previous', but it seemed a harsh step for receiving stolen property. Perhaps he was lying to me about the nature of his offence. At all events, Donnie disappeared from Shrewsbury some days before I did.

The other elements of induction consisted of visits to the library, the chapel and the gym. I had been told by someone who works in the probation service that morally dubious material doesn't make it to prison libraries, but that did not seem to be the case. The small stock of books contained a fair amount of horror and sci-fi and lots of crime, including true crime. The library even had Michael Dibdin's *Dirty Tricks* – an enthralling read, but fairly subversive, I should have thought, from a Home Office perspective.

The weirdest part of 'induction' was our visit to the gym on the afternoon of our first day. The gym was located through a heavy door on the ground floor of the prison, it was obviously well-equipped, and the master of ceremonies was the senior PE officer. He was a large, brutal looking man in his fifties with a missing front tooth, but he seemed kind enough. And he tried to reach out. Almost every word was qualified by 'fucking', and he addressed us as 'lads'.

The visit began with a talk about weight-lifting, correct posture demonstrated by a beefy young prisoner with a badge saying 'gym assistant'. He was another one who suffered from itchy nuts – in the intervals between lifting weights, he would grope deep into his joggers for a protracted scratch. The demonstration was reinforced by a fifteen-minute video on how to lift heavy objects.

This was followed by a rapid demonstration of how to put someone into 'the rescue position' and how to give the kiss of life and administer heart massage. We had to practise the rescue position on each other, but were given a dummy (head and torso only) – each 'fucking dummy worth two hundred fucking quid'– for the kiss of life and heart massage. This was a relief, since I was paired with Donnie.

When I was taken back to my cell, the screw escorting me noted my bewilderment and explained that the first-aid course was given in the hope that the druggies would be able to save each other's lives on the outside when they overdosed. We all got certificates (signed by the senior PE officer) – one was called a 'basic induction to weight-training award', the other bore the heading 'Heartstart UK' and confirmed that I had 'attended a course in emergency life support'. Unfortunately, I don't remember any of it.

Chapter Eleven
Shrewsbury: another world

My first few days in Shrewsbury were passed in a sort of torpor. I was constantly drowsy and my concentration was extremely weak. If I switched on the TV, my attention wandered immediately. During the induction visit to the prison chaplaincy, I fell asleep as the clergyman was in full flow. I guess it must have been shock. Maybe depression too. But I was functional – I was able to make phone calls and write letters.

After that, my state of mind improved. I got a bucket and mop and cleaned my cell; I started reading books and watching TV and keeping a journal of my impressions of prison life. This was mainly a question of time to adjust and cope, but a major factor was also that my nightmare scenarios of ostracism and bullying by the prison staff and the other inmates had proved unfounded.

Let me start with the screws. I owe a lot to the governor of Shrewsbury and a handful of the prison officers. That I did not have to share a cell for most of my time in the prison was a tremendous boon. I had assumed that it would only be for the first night, but it became clear over the next few days that it was 'policy' to keep me alone unless the prison became full. As a result, I remained in one of the 'reception' cells on the ground floor instead of being moved to a higher landing.

I was grateful for that, but I'm sure there were good pragmatic considerations behind this treatment as well as kindness. The prison authorities at Shrewsbury seemed very concerned about the danger of self-harm among the prisoners, and letting me have the single cell was an obvious way of reducing the risk in my case. There was also great concern about bullying and intimidation and, as a middle-aged 'first-timer', I was probably perceived as especially vulnerable to that, but I was not the only prisoner to have a single cell.

About half a dozen of the screws occasionally opened my cell door for a brief chat. It was obvious that they wanted me to know that they sympathised with me as fellow motorists. One advised me to appeal against the three-year driving ban imposed on me as it was self-evidently excessive, and another told me that 'anyone who says that what happened to you couldn't have happened to any driver doesn't live in the real world'.

He also made the point that I had been imprisoned but I hadn't been 'disgraced'. The concept of 'disgrace' had long since ceased to have much meaning for me, but I was touched by the goodwill behind his words.

Let me not exaggerate. I am talking about a small number of prison officers here. Most of the screws were as indifferent or brusque to me as to the other inmates. They were a mixed bunch. Few of them were young, many were overweight and most of them were heavy smokers. Giles and Mary (not their real names) represented the two extremes. Giles was the identikit liberal, the Mr Barraclough of Shrewsbury gaol. He told me he had never met a prisoner with no good in him, paused, considered and then added – 'Well, I suppose there was one who was completely evil, at least where women and children were concerned.' That sounded fairly hair-raising, and I did not seek elaboration. Giles was the only prison officer ever to put 'Mr.' in front of my surname when addressing me. Then there was Mary, a big, beefy woman unpopular with the inmates. She always managed to be unpleasant in some way or another, snapping and snarling at all around her.

There may be a much darker side which I never saw but, on the whole, I left Shrewsbury with a fairly positive impression of the prison authorities. The physical environment was appalling, but the regime, perhaps thanks to the governor, did not seem particularly harsh. The atmosphere was surprisingly relaxed and the relations between screws and inmates much better than you would have expected. I heard several inmates say that 'most of the screws in here aren't too bad'. There was occasional cheekiness from the prisoners and brusqueness from the screws, but the whole set-up made me think of the relationship between schoolmasters and roguish schoolchildren − a reflection perhaps of how young most of the prisoners were.

Which brings me to my fellow inmates. One screw told me that most of them were 'scumbags' and that seventy-five per cent of them were drug addicts. Drugs were certainly at the heart of life in Shrewsbury jail − getting them, talking about them, thinking about them. And thieving and sponging become second nature to druggies. Donnie was a good example − he was incapable of speech without an accompanying attempt at cadging. I used to give him a daily chocolate bar just to go away (I had plenty and never touched the stuff).

From the perspective of society as a whole, they probably were 'scumbags', but I was well treated by the other prisoners. As with the screws, I never had any contact with most of the prisoners, so I am talking about a small minority. They were perhaps curious about me just as I was curious about them. I was a bit exotic from their point of view – I was from the south, I was middle class and middle aged and I wasn't a drug addict. And my case had been on the news – though few of them spoke about it. Those who did were sympathetic. Ronnie told me that my imprisonment was unjust – or, as he put it, 'sending you down was a right liberty'. Frank said that another prisoner had been supporting my imprisonment 'for the sake of the families', but that he had defended me, asserting that 'he shouldn't be doing bird; he's got to live with it.' But such expressions of opinion were rare. Very few of the prisoners I spoke to referred to my case – in their eyes, I was in the shit like them and there was no more to say.

Ronnie and Frank were two of the inmates I met during exercise, my main opportunity of the day for social contact. They were both in their thirties and in prison for burglary. And they were both into drugs. Ronnie said that he wanted to give up drugs and was on the waiting list for a six-month stint in a drugs rehabilitation prison unit (he was doing three years). They spoke very openly about their drug addiction, and Frank referred to the agony of coming off drugs the first time he had been in prison. He was particularly graphic when talking about the sleeplessness – banging his head against the cell wall, shouting, 'I've got to sleep!'

One prison officer told me that there were so many drugs in the prison because the addicts hid the stuff up their backsides and the screws were not allowed to search digitally when they were admitted to prison. I was sceptical, but the point was confirmed by Billie, another of my acquaintances from the cage. He was only doing three weeks but had no intention of going without his heroin while he was inside. Billie needed a fix every six hours – coming off heroin was like having flu with aches and shivering, he said, only ten times worse. He had guessed he would be sentenced to prison and had come prepared. Billie had ten days supply of heroin up his arse plus 100 mezadrone tablets – in prison, they only give you two tablets a day, he claimed, and you need about forty to feel OK.

Even so, he was going to run out and I was surprised when he offered me some heroin (not then and there, obviously), but he explained that he would be more than all right as he had a lot of 'mates' in the prison. He had thought about putting a syringe up his bum as well, but decided against – he would have to burn and inhale while in prison. On the outside, he lived by shoplifting – his main line was stealing litre bottles of scotch from supermarkets and selling them to pubs for £10 each.

Billie was twenty-six and claimed to have been a hero-in addict for ten years. He did not conform to your normal picture of a druggie. He wasn't skinny and he didn't look ill at all. But I knew quite independently from his cellmate that he wasn't pulling my leg about his habits. In contrast to Billie, most of the druggies were instantly recognisable. You could spot them above all from their teeth. Frank (himself no model of successful dentistry) claimed that hard drugs destroy the teeth, and a high proportion of the young men around the prison bore him out. Brown, discoloured, partially rotted teeth as well as gaps were pretty well the norm.

Another addict was my one and only cellmate at Shrewsbury, Tony, who arrived on my last night when the prison reached overflowing point and every mattress was required. Around eight in the evening, the cell door opened and Tony was thrown into my cell. The word 'thrown' is apt, since it was just like you see in the movies – the prisoner propelled into the cell with a forceful shove and left glaring in aggrieved mode at the closing metal door. He was quite unfriendly at first, but later explained that this was not 'personal' – he was merely furious that the screws had not put him in the same cell as his 'mate', who had been admitted at the same time as him. Once he had got over that, he became quite chatty and was very keen to defend the reputation of druggies. He told me at once that he was a 'smackhead' and urged me not to believe 'everything you hear about heroin addicts – it's not about assaulting grannies.' Most addicts were God-fearing people, he asserted, who made an honourable living from shoplifting – strictly no grannies. His whole life seemed to revolve around drugs. We watched TV, but he couldn't take an interest in anything other than the two documentaries about drugs which happened to be on that night.

The druggies seemed mostly to be serving three to twelve months and had often been to prison before. They were petty criminals caught in a perpetual cycle of theft and imprisonment. They were slaves of their addiction. But there were also guys like Dick for whom dishonesty had become second nature. He wasn't a druggie, he was instinctively crooked. 'I've got no excuse,' he told me, 'I've got an education; I'm just the black sheep of the family.' Dick had come a cropper because it was his invariable habit to fill his tank with petrol out of town with false number plates fitted and had on one occasion forgotten to remove them before he got home. I was impressed that Dick could be bothered to go to such lengths to obtain free petrol. In Ford, I came across a similar example of unnecessary but unsleeping dishonesty – a fraudster rolling in money for many years but who still took the trouble to 'go on the sick' and collect £56 a week in benefits. He intended to resume the practice as soon as he was released.

One thing we all had in common was a terror of long prison sentences. It was a subject we discussed often. Dick, Ronnie and Frank spoke of being able to take a couple of years, even three or four, but beyond that sentences threaten to break you. Ronnie pointed out to me a black prisoner, one of the cleaners and always cheerful despite his predicament. He had been caught red-handed dealing in large amounts of drugs and was facing twenty years – 'That's your life gone,' said Ronnie. I also met two young men, murderers doing life, who had both served about ten years and who needed to do another two or three before being eligible for parole. They both used the same expression: 'This place is doing my head in.'

I was well-treated by the prison authorities in Shrewsbury, but I never forgot that I was a prisoner. That's the first rule of survival in prison – there's them and there's us. It's a rule that comes pretty naturally – instinctively even – once you're in a prison cell. I'm sure that the most vicious behaviour can and does occur between prisoners, but my overriding experience was of natural solidarity and instinctive defiance. It was something that I admired and respected. I still do.

Chapter Twelve
Wandsworth

My transfer to a Cat D gaol took place in two stages, because health and safety regulations did not allow me to be transported from Shrewsbury to Ford in one day. The journey was therefore broken by a night at Wandsworth gaol in London. These transfers, I now learnt, are handled by 'Group 4 Security', a company that also runs some private prisons. Both journeys were slightly more comfortable than when I was taken from Stoke in that the seat was cushioned, so the numb-bum factor was less, but it was still a cramped and sticky trip. On the first day, I was oddly elated as the sweat box headed south. I was going home, away from the Midlands and all the disasters I associated with that region. I had not yet sampled Wandsworth or the exquisite *longueurs* of Ford.

The initial impression conveyed by 'Wanno', as the

prisoners call it, is of immense dimensions – huge walls and gates, barbed wire. The officers in reception were a mixed group – most were civil enough, but there were three massive, muscular men with a rough manner. Wanno was also the only prison of the three I visited where there was gesture towards the idea of anal search. I had been given my suit back when I left Shrewsbury in the morning, but I now had to change back into prison uniform for the night. As I undressed, I noticed that there was one officer standing behind me, apparently doing nothing in particular. When I took off my underpants, he craned his neck slightly forward and I could see that he was peering into a square mirror that rose about a foot off the floor behind me. It was tilted at a diagonal angle and presumably afforded a good view up the barrel of my bum. I thought: 'Not much of a job, looking up people's arseholes all day.'

In the long term, I had the prospect of more congenial employment than him, but that night Wanno gave me a glimpse up the arsehole of the British prison system. After reception, the new arrivals who, like me, were in transit to another prison were taken on a long, tortuous walk to C wing, the section of Wanno where remand prisoners are held. Wanno is (I'm told) one of the biggest 'local' prisons in Europe, and the wings all converge like the spokes of a giant wheel on one round, central area. In the middle of this central area is a large metal grille. On both the occasions that I passed through it, we were told by the screws not to step on the grille and to walk to its right. I learned later in Ford from prisoners who had done time in Wanno that inmates were always made to walk anti-clockwise around this central area, because 'it makes the time go more slowly'. It was, in other words, a good old English tradition like Morris dancing – but designed to torment prisoners rather than tourists.

As we walked through the prison on our way to C wing, association or dinner seemed to be in full swing in most places, and there were shouts and bustle everywhere. And every manner of man, of all ages and races. My cell on C wing was bigger and more recently painted than Shrewsbury, and it had a handbasin and toilet in a separate room. Such privacy was a privilege enjoyed on remand – in the rest of the prison, the toilet was behind a low screen in the cell, as in Shrewsbury.

But there wasn't much else to be said in favour of Wanno. En suite bathroom maybe, but it hadn't seen anything like cleaning fluid for a long time. There was no TV in the cell. The window could only be opened slightly because of the bars outside and the cell must be sweltering in real heat. (In Shrewsbury, the window opened inwards and wide.) The floor was utterly filthy and my socks picked up a film of sticky yellow slime within thirty minutes of arrival.

The worst thing was the lack of blinds or curtains, which meant that a yellowish light from a lamp outside shone into the cell all night. There was also constant clamour from B wing facing my cell – screaming, what might have been Islamic prayers, prisoners banging on the doors and window bars of their cells. The noise, the squalor of the cell, the sickly yellow light pouring in all night – those eighteen hours or so in Wanno were the most terrifying of my imprisonment.

It was mainly in the mind. No one was threatening towards me, and I would doubtless have adapted if obliged to stay in Wanno. I spent much of the night telling myself that I could and would tough it out through the next five weeks if the move to Ford never took place. I became quite paranoid during the witching hours on this point and was very relieved when a screw fetched me at 9.30 the next morning. I was right to be worried. I was a paranoiac in full suspicion of the facts. I didn't learn this till later, but in fact the sweat box booked to transfer prisoners often gets cancelled or 'postponed' for one reason or another.

I shared the cell with a remand prisoner called John, who had been in it for some time with a succession of transient cellmates. John was a drunk who had been sleeping rough for three years outside Liverpool Street Station after he had lost his job as a boat-builder somewhere on the south coast. He was still in touch with his mother and brother, and had lived a regular existence (sort of) before his arrest. He had used his social security benefits to buy prepared salads and drink from the supermarket and fast food from a burger bar, and he had had his fixed place to sleep on the street.

John was on remand for assaulting someone while drunk. He was thirty-nine, he told me, and was on medication 'for [his] nerves'. As well as tablets, he was given some pink liquid to drink each evening before dinner. He had drunken, sleepy eyes and was pretty drowsy most of the time. Tony seemed a dreamy, harmless soul (which he probably wasn't when drunk) and I did not feel threatened by him at all. I hope the system didn't shaft him too badly.

In Ford, I spoke to some prisoners who had been in Wanno and a few said that life there wasn't as bad as it seemed on a fleeting visit. The screws who had once allegedly stalked the prison with swastikas tattooed on their foreheads were long gone. These days, there were cells with TVs, even single cells, even some friendly screws. Maybe so, but for me, Wanno was the nearest thing to hell on earth that I've ever witnessed.

IV CAT D

Chapter Thirteen
Ford: the daily grind

The great bulk of my sentence, five weeks, was served in Ford open prison, but it has left a less vivid impression than my much shorter exposure to Cat B. Life in Shrewsbury and Wandsworth had been unreal, unlike anything I could have imagined. When I think back to Ford, I remember interminable weeks of squalor and boredom. My first ten days there consisted of weekends and 'induction', the last three and a half weeks of 'work' as an orderly in the education department, but all those dreary days appear indistinguishable in retrospect.

***

The main compound of the prison is surrounded by a wire fence, ten or twelve feet high perhaps, which bends inwards at the top to discourage attempts to climb over.

The centre of this compound is taken up by a large expanse of grass with a cricket pitch in the middle and a jogging track around its rim. Ford was an RAF base before it became a prison and is located on flat, low-lying land. You couldn't see much over the top of the perimeter fence, and my strongest recollection is of broad, overarching skies with elaborate cloud formations and often spectacular sunsets.

The core of the prison consists of A wing, a long two-storey building which accommodates most of the single cells for prisoners as well as the dining hall, the library and various offices. The rest of the accommodation for prisoners is in the fifteen or so long huts of B wing on the other side of the compound.

Finally, on the side facing the road are two modern buildings in red brick – the chapel, probation and education in one, reception and the visiting centre in the other. These are the flash, up-to-date parts of Ford and serve to give a false impression of what the prison is really like. They are the public face of the prison and mask the more sordid reality. I suspect that few visitors ever get taken anywhere else. Ford is a fur-coat-no-knickers sort of place.

The rest of the prison (which is surrounded by another fence) lies across the road through the gates, and contains the governor's office, 'estates' (the potting shed, vegetable beds etc.) and other work places. Most of the prisoners had jobs there, but I cannot have paid more than three or four flying visits to this section of the prison during my whole time in Ford.

Like all prisons, Ford operated according to rigid timetables. There were three meals in the dining hall – at 8, 11.30 and 4.30. 'Roll check' (when you have to stand by your bed while a screw makes sure you are there) occurred four times a day: 8, 1 p.m. (11.30 a.m. at week-ends), 6 and 9. You were supposed to stay in your cell or hut from 9 p.m. until eight the next morning. Most activities had their clearly allocated slots. You collected your mail between 11.30 and 12.15 every day except Sunday and exchanged your clothing every Thursday or Friday between 6 and 8.

***

Jobs for inmates are in short supply at Cat B, but an open prison is meant to be 'a working prison', and all inmates are supposed to be engaged in work or study/training or a combination of the two. At Ford, the second of these three options was not available and no prisoner was allowed to spend more than fifty per cent of his time on education or training.

The problem was that there was not enough work to

go around. The solution adopted was to employ three men to do the work of one. This suited the inmates very well. Apart from a handful who worked zealously either to combat boredom or to gain brownie points for parole purposes, the great majority of prisoners wanted to do as little work as possible. As far as we were concerned, this was forced labour, and dragging our feet was a way of saying 'fuck you' to the prison system. Most of the work was also extremely tedious. Being allocated to 'assembly', a sort of mini-factory where various small gadgets were put together, was particularly feared among the inmates.

I was employed as an 'education orderly'. It was a position that probably only offered enough work for one person, but there were three orderlies and I was very much surplus to requirements. By the time I started to work, I only had another three and a half weeks to serve and something had to be done with me.

What does an education orderly do? For me, it was largely a case of manning the desk in the entrance hall while reading a book or writing letters. I was rarely disturbed – just being there to deal with the infrequent enquiries in person or by phone was enough. The orderlies also marked the numeracy and literacy tests that each weekly intake of prisoners had to sit, kept the class registers and delivered the 'call-up slips' informing prisoners when they had been allocated to a particular course. There were more complicated duties involving computer records, but I was there too briefly to become involved in that.

The work was exquisitely boring, but there was a lot going for the education department. It was recently built and provided a warm, clean and dry perch. You rarely saw a screw. My job brought me into contact with a much wider range of prisoners than would otherwise have been the case. With a few exceptions, the teachers were pleasant, even diffident in some cases, in their dealings with the orderlies. I can think of no other posting that would have suited me better, except perhaps for the library.

I found it difficult to form any judgement about the quality or value of the courses offered by the education department. They were an odd combination of the vocational and the character-building. The first category was the largest – IT, literacy and numeracy, cookery, 'small business', that sort of thing. I got the impression that most prisoners quite liked these courses, and the same went for inmates taking A levels, OU degrees and other qualifications under the 'distance learning' programme.

The prisoners also appeared to enjoy the recreational evening classes in craft, art and pottery. I wonder, though, about the character-building element. Courses in anger control are offered in most prisons, usually under the name of 'enhanced thinking' (though that isn't the term used in Ford). Like joining AA or NA (Narcotics Anonymous), the idea is to make prisoners less prone to reoffend, but participation in such courses is often part of an inmate's 'sentence plan', a condition for getting early release in one form or another, and this breeds a certain cynicism.

***

There's a lot that can be said in favour of Ford. Above all, there is the absence of twenty-three-hour bang up and the freedom to walk around in the open air much of the time. It was an extraordinary relief to be there after the claustrophobic world of Cat B. What else does Ford have going for it? Well, you can wear your own clothes when you are not working, and there were few problems about having personal items sent to you or handed in on visits. As a result, Jannie was able to supply me with stamps, writing paper, a combined radio and cassette player, books, proper shaving gear and much else besides. The facilities for sport and physical activity are good. So is the library, which has been recently refurbished and holds a respectable collection of books, newspapers and magazines.

What could most definitely not be said in favour of Ford were the living conditions in B Wing. Most of the huts there are what the authorities at Ford call 'billets'. In normal parlance, they would be described as dormitories containing sixteen beds, eight each side of a shared aisle. The huts also have a small kitchen with a sink and kettle, a table and a few chairs. Beyond the kitchen lie the indelicacies of the communal toilet (two shower cubicles, two WCs, two urinals and six washbasins).

All prisoners initially go into a billet, supposedly for a short period, before transferring to a single cell – first without, but ultimately with a TV. That was the theory. In practice, Ford was grossly overcrowded so you had to wait three to four weeks for the transfer. And if your shot at a single cell came up less than two weeks before your release, you weren't transferred at all. The outcome was that I spent the whole five weeks in a billet (Hut O, 'berth' sixteen).

The hut was long and low, a white prefab. The sixteen living spaces were separated by a partition reaching to head height, and each had a table, a small wooden locker (with a key), a bed and a window (no curtain, but

I improvised with a towel). Illumination in the dormitory area was provided by six strip lights on the ceiling. The one above me only came on if I climbed onto the bed and twiddled with a knob on the side of the strip.

My berth, number sixteen, was next to the kitchen, the payphone and the toilet, and I was sometimes unaware of who was sleeping at the other end of the dormitory (prisoners were being moved in and out all the time). That was lucky for me. It placed me close to the amenities and somewhat shielded from the snoring and farting that punctuated the night. Even so, it was a noisy place in the evenings – there were plenty of radios banging out rock music and a group of inmates who liked to play cards or board games (both borrowed from the library) in the kitchen.

Other inmates were less insulated. Sanjay had a bed in the middle of the dormitory and his snoring was so thunderous that he exiled himself to the kitchen. As I passed on my way for a pee in the dead of night, I often saw him curled in a foetal position on the kitchen table.

Everything about the dormitory was second-rate and shabby – the mattresses were lumpy and dirty, the tables often had wobbly legs, the key to my locker could only be turned after learning a variety of cunning manipulations. And the insulation was terrible. Ford is on flat land close to the sea, and the hut was very cold. We had been supplied with two blankets, neither made of wool, and both crocheted with some flimsy material (one middle-aged inmate observed that they reminded him of the old string vests of his youth). This proved a disadvantage during a cold snap in early September, when we spent a week or so sleeping with all our clothes piled on top of our blankets.

***

But the highlight of Hut O was the toilet, where the stink of piss and rot was never entirely absent. The floor of the WC closest to the showers was constantly wet. That, however, was the bog with a functional lock on the door. Its companion had a reasonably dry floor, but a broken lock, leaving you with a choice between wet feet (or worse) with a locked door and crapping behind a door that was a few inches ajar. I oscillated between the two, but generally plumped for the dry feet option and paid the price in having prisoners push the door open on several occasions.

Sometimes the boot was on the other foot and I twice walked in on other inmates. The first time, it was a scrawny junkie called Chris, who suffered serious bowel problems by his own account. Chris reacted to my pushing the door open with a despairing wail of 'No, please'.

That showed a serious lack of cool, but Franciscus, a far more laid-back prisoner, displayed admirable grace under pressure in similar circumstances and merely said, 'Hey, slow down there, man.'

There seems to be an obsession in prison about brushing toilets. In Shrewsbury, there were notices above the johns in the cells urging the inmates to 'flush and brush' and the two cubicles in my billet at Ford had the same exhortation. The authorities at Ford were less generous with toilet paper than they were with sanitary advice. In Shrewsbury and Wandsworth, toilet paper was freely available. At Ford, bum paper was allocated by prisoner – each inmate received two rolls and one box of tissues a month. Apparently, the Home Office estimates that two is what a prisoner needs at a 'working prison', since he can do some of his shitting at his work place. Loo paper was consequently in short supply.

After I started as an orderly in the education department, I took the Home Office at its word and tried hard to time my daily shit for when I was working, often walking to the education department in the mornings with ever more desperate footsteps. In fact, bum paper was not kept in the prisoners' toilet of the education department, because any that was left there was rapidly nicked. Instead, the orderlies kept it in the filing cabinet behind their desk and inmates had to ask for it on their way to the bog and return it afterwards. Hence the graffito in the john – printed notice: 'PLEASE USE THE TOILET BRUSH PROVIDED' (that old obsession of the prison authorities again). Graffito: 'I'D RATHER USE TOILET PAPER.'

***

Unlike the Cat B prisons I'd been in, Ford had a dining hall. Meals were therefore a social event, though the effect was spoiled by having to queue for fifteen or twenty minutes to get your food – yet another manifestation of overcrowding. Can I find anything kind to say about the food? Well, the standard is probably not much below the general run of British institutional food, and after more than thirty years of eating in British university refectories, I was man enough to take it.

The dinners in Ford were usually tolerable. Lunch, on the other hand, was unspeakable – 'chicken rib burger' (sic) or pasta hoops in a sweet tomato sauce, that sort of thing. The hoops were particularly vile, especially when they were combined with a watery mashed potato. As in Shrewsbury, there were always Halal and vegetarian options. Most of the time, there was also a 'healthy eating' choice signified by a simple drawing of a round, smiling face. Sounds good, but the offering often struck me as eccentric – cheese and onion flan, and ('no, please', to quote Chris) 'seaburger'. Breakfast consisted of cereals and toast, Monday to Friday (or it did until the toaster broke down). Weekends brought a treat – a cooked breakfast. The choice was two of the following – scrambled egg, boiled egg, one sausage, one rasher of bacon. If you had two bacon rashers, you lost your egg, but fried bread was always plentiful.

Detergent was entirely absent from the dining hall and the hut. The inmates rinsed their cutlery under hot running water in the dining hall, but there was no scouring pad or washing-up liquid. This was in line with the sanitary conditions in the billets. I brought up the question of hygiene during induction week when the new intake had a meeting with two representatives of the Board of Visitors, a group that is meant to function as an independent watchdog on prison conditions. They were a world-weary pair, but they briefly perked up at this stage. Could it be that here was a case where they could do something about a point raised by a prisoner? No, they couldn't: on reflection, the older of the two visitors was sure the prison authorities would take the line that 'no one's died yet'. That said it all, and is one of the main reasons why I can feel no respect for Ford as an institution, its governor or his staff.

***

Like the prison authorities at Ford, I had a routine of sorts. I was getting out in five weeks, so there was no point in setting myself a serious body of work, but I pursued my classical studies diligently and kept a prison journal. That still left a lot of time to kill. My day had a variety of highpoints. The lunch break was for collecting and reading my mail. The hour or two after the 6 p.m. roll check was for reading the newspapers in the library. After the 9 p.m. curfew, I would read (novels mostly) and write letters or my journal before listening to audio books or music on the earphones of my radio as I dozed off between midnight and one o'clock. Most nights, I had enough phonecard units left to speak briefly to Jannie around eleven.

I also spent a lot of time walking the road that ran just inside the perimeter fence of the main compound, alone or in company. This was a popular activity among prisoners and there were often so many of them on the road that we must have resembled a mass trespass by a crowd of committed ramblers. I did a lot of thinking on these walks and also a lot of chatting. I probably had more conversation with other prisoners out walking than I did in the billet or the education department.

It was a dull and monotonous life, and the almost

total lack of privacy was debilitating. But I found my techniques for fighting the boredom, for surviving. We all did.

Chapter Fourteen
Ford: strangers and brothers

In Cat B, the screws who let you in and out of your cell are your main point of contact with the world. At Ford, days could go by without ever speaking to a warder. I didn't have a single conversation with a prison officer in Ford except about matters of the most purely practical kind, and I never witnessed any natural human contact between screws and inmates there. As a result, the screws at Ford didn't have much of an impact on me. Some seemed quite pleasant, others less so.

I didn't see anything that could be interpreted as bullying or intimidation by the screws. Rudeness and casual nastiness – like refusing to accept a canteen order form because it was handed in thirty minutes late – but nothing heavy. Their attitude to the inmates seemed detached and indifferent.

What did strike me about the warders at Ford was

their laziness. They weren't off their backsides often. Visits to the B wing office generally unearthed a bunch of screws lolling about, watching TV or reading a newspaper. In this respect, they provided a role model that we prisoners were eager to follow. My overriding impression of the authorities was that they were mean-spirited, but hardly proactive. It was a regime of pettiness ameliorated by indolence.

**

Before I left Shrewsbury, Giles – the kindest of the screws there – said to me that 'you'll be among gentlemen like yourself' at Ford, with a sprinkling of 'rogues', and 'a few ordinary lads like the ones here'. This wasn't really true. Ford was not crammed with gentlemen-crooks doing their porridge and dreaming of the offshore accounts waiting for them on the outside. There certainly was a substantial middle-class contingent, and the average age of the prisoners was much higher than in Shrewsbury. But it seemed to me that a majority of the prisoners were working class and convicted not of fraud but of theft, assault, drug dealing or smuggling and the like (the usual, in other words). There were also a fair number of junkies, though they were in a better physical state than the Shrewsbury ones.

There were lots of blacks in Ford, and a fair number of Asians too. I also came across French and Portuguese prisoners. I saw no evidence of overt racial hostility. Every skin pigmentation imaginable, except for far eastern, was represented in my billet, and we all rubbed along well enough. Away from the billets and the work places, however, each ethnic group tended to keep to itself, and to a lesser extent the same voluntary self-segregation also applied to class. But I am describing tendencies, not absolute barriers. The prisoners with whom I trudged the perimeter fence were mainly white, middle-class conmen, but included all sorts. The group was created far more by age than by class or colour.

An example that makes the point was Paddy Plonker, who was both working class and of mixed race, but above the magic age of thirty-five. He was incredibly thick. By his own telling, he got nicked because he didn't bugger off when the police told him to go. He was doing six months for theft as a result. Once, on a cold and windy day, as the shambling ramblers strolled the perimeter, a flock of birds passed overhead, flying in V formation, as they often do, with one trailing behind. When Paddy spotted them, he exclaimed, 'Look at those birds! They're flying together because they're cold.' After a pause, Lennie replied, 'That one flying by himself must be fucking freezing.' But Paddy was kind. He worked in the kitchen and shared such treats as were available with his friends. As Lennie said, Paddy was, 'a fuckwit with a heart of gold'.

**

I was surprised by how many of the inmates in Ford had a woman in their lives, but I shouldn't have been. I had merely made the simplistic assumption that a criminal lifestyle was unlikely to be compatible with relationships that could survive the strains of imprisonment. Instead, the opposite seemed true. A prisoner cherishes the ties that bind him to a woman on the outside, and – what is perhaps more unexpected – the woman generally sticks by him. From my berth, I heard the whispered endearments every night from the payphone in the hall a few feet away.

A young inmate whom I christened Goofy because of his appearance and limited brain power was particularly active on the phone. He made long calls every night to a lady he addressed as 'Gorgeous'. Bob preferred writing. He had done three years already on a long sentence for what sounded (and that was by his own account) like a very nasty case of assault and told me that he had thousands of 'love letters' from his wife. On a recent family visit, he had informed her that when he got out, 'You'll be off your feet all day, my girl; your fanny will be glowing red.' When I asked him how his wife had responded, he said she had merely replied, 'Don't speak like that in front of your mum, Bob.'

But it wasn't all roses. Ben got dumped over the phone the night before his release, while Brian rang home every evening for a daily row with his wife, his voice whinging and querulous – like Ian Beale's in *EastEnders*. And in the education department, one of the inmates selected for a 'parenting skills' course turned up – muscular, heavily tattooed arms, cropped hair, bullet-shaped head – and told me as he loomed over the orderlies' desk that he didn't want to attend. 'No point, mate. The wife wrote me a Dear John letter and won't let me see the kids.'

At Ford, inmates were entitled to four two-hour visits a month. The visits were two hours in principle, but less in practice. They always started ten or fifteen minutes late and finished five minutes early. All prisoners were frisked after a visit. They could also be strip searched, but that never happened to me. It goes without saying that these visits were a vital lifeline for prisoners, but they were distressing too. I often felt vaguely dejected after a visit, more acutely alive to my isolation in an alien world.

Prisoners often pinned up photos from girlie mags on

their notice-boards, but they needed to be careful. Nowadays, prison regulations stipulate that 'offensive' (i.e. sexist or racist) material may not be displayed. Gary, who moved into the berth opposite mine a few days before my release, was told to take down half of the eight photos torn from magazines that he had put up. They were all photos of topless girls (the screw had allowed mere cleavage to survive). 'They were some of my best ones,' Gary grumbled.

It is often said that homosexuality is widespread in prisons, but I didn't notice any evidence of homosexual activity. Nor was there much sign of homophobia. A few of the prisoners in Ford were effeminate, but that did not seem to attract animosity towards them. Real hostility focused on sex offenders, the 'nonces' held in special 'segregation units'. There were such units at Shrewsbury and Wandsworth, but not at Ford, so I assume sex offenders don't get sent to Cat D prisons. That did not prevent the frequent expression of irrational and undiscriminating hatred of 'nonces' by inmates of Ford.

Apart from slagging off nonces, there was little talk among the prisoners at Ford about sex-related matters. Sex was treated as a private matter, your business only. The same attitude applied to drugs.

***

All prisons operate a 'mandatory drug testing' programme, both on a random basis and when there are special reasons (like 'reasonable suspicion') for ascertaining whether an inmate has drugs in his bloodstream. This is what prisoners call the 'piss test'. I was never tested, but I saw other inmates being summoned to provide a urine sample now and then. Ford (like Wandsworth) had 'drug-free wings'. Shrewsbury did not, presumably because all the prisoners, apart from those in the 'segregation unit', were accommodated in one great barn of a building.

I never quite understood what drug-free wings were meant to achieve, but I think the idea was the prisoners committed to avoiding drug use were to be accommodated together on discrete corridors, which non-residents were forbidden to enter, shielded from the blandishments of potential suppliers. In return, they had to agree to regular piss tests to ensure that they were sticking to the straight and narrow.

No one ever drew attention to the grotesque aspects of providing special accommodation for inmates who wanted to avoid drugs in prisons which are supposed to be entirely drug-free in the first place. But of course British prisons are riddled with drugs in practice. Compared with Shrewsbury, the proportion of inmates who had been or were still on drugs seemed fairly small, but there were certainly drugs in Ford. I heard many stories of packets containing drugs being thrown over the fence by loved ones lurking in the bushes outside, but I doubt there was much truth behind them.

The only drug I actually witnessed being used was cannabis. I often saw joints being smoked in the toilet or the doorway of my billet. That was just part of the scenery. Druggies and non-druggies treated such matters on a live-and-let-live basis.

***

Even if many of the inmates had convictions for crimes of violence, there was little sense of threat or menace – I always felt safe in Ford. Most prisoners were courteous enough in their dealings with each other, and there was a lot of kindness and solidarity. Lending or giving tobacco, milk, sugar, biscuits to other prisoners were very common. I also liked the sense of unspoken defiance, the refusal to surrender to the prison authorities.

While marking the weekly tests in the education department, I was struck by the low literacy level among the prisoners in Ford. About forty per cent failed. The pass rate for numeracy was higher – cons need to know their sums, especially how to work out their percentage. But lack of literacy skills is not the same as stupidity, and many inmates could be shrewd and witty raconteurs even if they were short on formal education.

I enjoyed listening, some of the time at least, but an awful lot of bullshit was spoken in prison. It is a bottomless well of false information. Just about anything a fellow inmate told you about prison turned out to be mistaken. The best tall stories concerned going over the fence. It was easy to get out of Ford, and it was claimed that a couple of prisoners absconded every night. The perimeter fence certainly seemed to show signs of sagging in many places.

A brief jaunt down to Tesco in Ford village was said to be more common than escape. A prisoner would go over the fence equipped with cash that had been smuggled in to buy vodka and cigarettes for a group of inmates and then return, receiving a commission for his trouble. There was one tale of a prisoner waiting his turn at the checkout who turned round to find a screw behind him in the queue. This surely must be apocryphal, and I suspect that nearly all the other Tesco stories were untrue.

I'm only aware of two escapes to my certain knowledge, and I doubt that there were many in reality, but it was a very agreeable fantasy. I often speculated about how I would do it – would I climb the fence (probably not, too corpulent and unfit), walk through the gate or slip out next to the potting shed in 'estates' (where I was told you could have a car waiting to speed you away)? For some reason, helicopters often seemed to pass over Ford, and every time I liked to toy with the thought that a rope ladder would descend to the cricket pitch and an inmate climb up it while I cheered him on.

There were many ways in which prisoners could be quite tiresome. Farting in the billet is a case in point. A lot of the residents of Hut O were ripping them off day and night, but the champion was Mad Max or 'Captain Methane', as Lennie dubbed him. Max bragged that he had convictions for 'eight crimes of violence'. On this occasion, however, he claimed to be unjustly imprisoned. He had been rescuing a damsel in distress outside a pub at closing time, but she had run off by the time the police turned up to find Max kicking the shit out of her assailant. I could see why the magistrates might have had trouble about buying this story.

Max's appearance was distinctive – shaven head, wispy blond goatee and an alarmingly lazy eye. To quote Lennie again, 'That poor bastard wouldn't stand much chance in a line up.' He played his radio (football or rock) very loud and seemed to have no other interests beyond sport, drink and sex. He confided that he was planning to do 'a lot of wanking' once he got his single cell. Unfortunately, he was less inclined to defer his pleasures when it came to flatulence and broke wind with startling frequency and volume. Max took great pride in his long, yodelling farts.

Conversation could often be tedious, mine included. We had the same discussions time and again: dissecting the minutiae of life in Ford, the iniquities of the prison regime and so on. Nothing else seemed equally real and immediate. Prisoners were obsessive, chattering endlessly about their chances of obtaining early release through parole or electronic tagging. Appeals against conviction or sentence and the incompetence of lawyers were other popular topics.

My overwhelming impression of my fellow prisoners is how ordinary they were, how much like all the other people you meet in everyday life. If these were evil men, it was not obvious to the naked eye. Many of them were doubtless serial offenders, but they had the same habits and tastes as most people. What marked them out was that they belonged to that section of the population that society is accustomed to imprisoning and that spells in the pokey were a part of their lifestyles.

Chapter Fifteen
Ford: states of mind

Imprisonment is a vile and degrading experience and I hated every minute of it. That is hardly surprising. Imprisonment is the worst thing that British society does to its members and it had just happened to me. I could have received much harsher treatment from the court, and in retrospect my imprisonment seems like a fleeting episode in my life, but it did not feel like a short sentence at the time. They were long days.

Most people who have never been locked up would probably regard physical confinement as the worst aspect of prison life, and it must be devastating for inmates serving long sentences, but I did not find the limited freedom of movement a great psychological burden. Far worse was the humiliation, the indignity of it, the shock of moving from a way of life where I had received a modicum of courtesy and respect to the status of a prisoner. Allied to this was the lack of authority and control over your own life. In principle, inmates do have rights. In practice, you feel utterly powerless. Only the ability to think your own thoughts cannot be taken away from you.

I also found the lack of privacy, the filth and the squalor of Hut O1 profoundly dispiriting – though they also helped to keep my sense of outrage and defiance aflame and in that sense were good for my morale. And it's worth mentioning here that it wasn't only fussy, middle-aged men like me who regarded the billets as the pits. All the prisoners hated them.

⁕

I spent a lot of time thinking about the future while I was in Ford. I often considered the practicality of a new life after my release – one less governed by work and ambition, more focused on family and recreation. I was, in short, dreaming of becoming a quality of life man.

At the same time, I was determined that the enemy – the police, the CPS, the legal and prison systems – would not turn me into a harmless wimp, and such notions of striking a better balance between work and the intimate sphere coexisted with bitterness, anger and a renewed sense of alienation from British society while I was in

Ford. Once again, I toyed with the idea of emigration after my release, even though I knew that it was entirely impractical. Once again, dreams of an impossible, an unattainable revenge filled my mind.

To adapt a quote from somewhere or other, God was dead, and I was feeling a bit tired myself. Nothing was consistent in my thinking while I was in Ford. Alienation rubbed along side by side with a desire to make a greater contribution to British society through involvement in the community. Ideas of leading a less stressful life coexisted with endless plans for new projects of historical research that I would undertake after I was released. It was a curious mental world of overlapping and partially contradictory fantasies.

**

I was sometimes dejected, but on the whole my spirits held up quite well while I was in Ford. I was greatly assisted in this respect by support from the great world outside. The emotional burden of my incarceration was immensely lightened by the many letters I received while I was inside. They came in the first instance from my family – above all Jannie, who thought I should have a letter every day, however brief; my sons and my Danish relatives through blood or marriage. What I had not expected was the steady flow of letters from friends, colleagues at work (including virtually every member of my own department) and fellow historians at home and abroad whom I had encountered over the years. Many of them wrote repeatedly, and some were from individuals I had not seen for years or with whom I was very slightly acquainted. On average, I got three or four letters a day while I was in Ford – some were a few brief lines of support, others in addition were long and chatty.

I was tremendously moved by these letters and devoted a lot of my time in Ford to answering them. I was also astonished to be the recipient of so much friendship and goodwill, and I remain deeply grateful for that. This is one of the few positive lessons I've learnt from my trial and imprisonment – never let awkwardness hold you back; always say or write some words of sympathy.

Most astonishing of all were the messages and letters from strangers. They were prompted by the magnitude and nature of the media reports about my case. As with my conviction, the press coverage of my sentencing was all neutral in tone, except for the *Sun*, which printed a moderately hostile but very brief article. But the decisive factor in persuading strangers to offer sympathy was Carol Midgley's interview with me in the *Times*. Carol wrote to me in Ford to say that many letters and phone calls had come in to the *Times* with offers of help, ranging from sending me books on Ancient Greek (Carol had mentioned my classical studies in her article) to enquiries about organising a petition calling for my release. I was particularly touched by a letter sent to the judge through the *Times*, which asked him to 'reconsider whether a custodial sentence is really appropriate in this case'. The letter was from a lady who had lost her husband in a motor accident ten years earlier. The other driver had been at fault, but the author of the letter had never felt that prison was the right punishment.

I know that some of the letters sent to the *Times* or my former home address, and even to my work address, never reached me, so I take this opportunity to thank anyone who wrote but did not receive a reply for their moral support.

***

The outside world was not only a source of support. It also contained potential threats – both from the prosecution and from my employers. My greatest anxiety focused on the possibility that the prosecution might appeal against my sentence. Both Alan and Annette had assured me that such an appeal was unlikely, but the fear of it remained a black, brooding cloud that poisoned every moment I spent in Ford. Even after I learnt that the prosecution had to appeal within twenty-one days of sentence, I remained consumed with fears that they had secretly done so and that I would not get out on 27 September. I need not have worried about this last point – I was forgetting that the legal process is a streetcar named delay. Even if the prosecution had appealed, I would still have been released on 27 September and would have lived under the shadow of renewed imprisonment for the same offence until the case was heard many months later.

The right of the prosecution to appeal against sentence is a relatively recent addition to the British legal system. It rests, I suppose, on the assumption that some judges who impose excessively lenient sentences are at large within the tentacles of the legal system. For all I know, this may be true, but the prosecution's right of appeal against sentence is a stalking-horse for a right to appeal against jury acquittals – which is what I assume our politicians really want, if they can't abolish jury trials altogether. At all events, the danger that the prosecution may appeal against sentence functions as a cruel form of double jeopardy for the convicted prisoner.

In comparison with the threat of a prosecution appeal against sentence, the risk that my employers might attempt to dismiss me from my post seemed a trifling matter. I was pretty confident that my sentence was too short for any such move to be successful, but I wanted it in black and white. About a fortnight after my conviction, I learnt the line that college was adopting through a letter sent to me at my home address by the 'human resources' division (as personnel is now called at college). The letter stated that I would be deemed to be on unpaid leave of absence during the period of my imprisonment. I would be 'expected' to return to work on the cessation of my research leave on 1 October unless my release was delayed beyond that date.

So far, so good. There would clearly be no attempt to dismiss me. But the letter contained a gratuitous and spiteful concluding sentence which I interpreted as code, a way of saying that my interview with the *Times* had been noted and resented by college management. If my interpretation is correct, what really niggled was that Carol described me as uncertain where I stood with college and wrote about the way I had sorted the belongings in my office so that they could be more easily cleared by my family in the event of my dismissal. Whatever the motive, it was distasteful conduct at a time when my position, locked up in a prison cell, could not have been weaker. Jannie saw the letter before I did and was equal to the occasion. She wrote an excellent reply, taking exception to the concluding sentence and, to my surprise, extracted an apology. All this soured my mood, but the main point was that my job was safe. The fact that I was in bad odour with college management didn't seem very significant from the perspective of prison.

**

There was a lot of confusion during my first days of imprisonment over whether I would be eligible for Home Detention Curfew (popularly known as 'electronic tagging'). It eventually transpired that had I been sentenced to three calendar months, I could in principle have got two weeks on the tag, but that ninety days was less than three months and that I was consequently ineligible. I was not too upset about this. Getting out of Ford two weeks earlier would have been splendid, but at least my home was not violated by the intrusion of officialdom sniffing around and installing electronic equipment. In any case, the point was probably academic – I doubt the probation office at Ford would have processed the paperwork quickly enough to get me out before the forty-five days were up. I certainly knew several inmates who got the tag later than they should have done or not at all.

I was released on Thursday, 27 September at 8.30 in the morning. The previous day, I had been forced by a particularly officious screw to sign a form undertaking to refrain from handling firearms for five years. Every prisoner doing three months or more had to sign the form, the screw told me, and the authorities at Ford regarded my ninety days as the equivalent of three months. That was a bit rich considering that I had been declared ineligible for the tag on the grounds that ninety days is less than three months, but I wasn't going to endanger my release by quibbling.

As I walked into reception to undergo the formalities of release, I encountered one of the more unpleasant teachers of the education department arriving for work. We exchanged dirty looks. Inside reception, there were two screws handling releases. I got my rail travel warrant and my £56 discharge grant and signed for my belongings. After I had packed them into a black refuse bag provided by the prison, I walked through the door onto the road outside. Neither I nor the two screws said a word as I did so.

Chapter Sixteen
Epilogues

I went back to work within days of my release. The letter from college had stated that I was 'expected' to return to work on 1 October 2001 when my research leave came to an end, and I was not going to give my employers any excuse for withholding more of my pay. I was also anxious to face the world again, to find out how I would be received by rank-and-file members of college.

In fact, the welcome proved to be warm and generous – not only from the teachers and students in my own department but also from academic staff in other departments and from some of the manual and administrative workers employed at college. I was very moved.

I continued to get letters from strangers. A few were eccentric, but the letters were overwhelmingly sympathetic, and only two were unpleasant. One was from solicitors representing my ex-wife, who demanded the retrospective payment of the child maintenance I had been unable to provide while my salary was stopped. The other was from an Edinburgh cyclist, who took it upon himself to write in a spidery hand in order to call me a murderer.

Despite all the support I received, I was subject to re-entry problems for the first few months after my release. Every time I heard a police siren, I feared for a moment they were coming for me under some pretext or other. I was mildly surprised to be treated with courtesy by shopkeepers, ticket inspectors and the like – it was as if the disempowerment I had suffered in prison was branded on my forehead and I expected it to infect the behaviour of everyone I encountered. All that proved short-lived, but even now I am sometimes prey to irrational anxieties. Because I was convicted, the police are entitled to keep the fingerprints I gave at Chesterfield in May 2000 for the rest of my life, and I experience moments of fear that they will use them to fit me up for some new offence.

I remain deeply troubled by the three deaths that occurred in that horrifying accident through an act of stupidity on my part. Three innocent lives cut short, three human beings full of hopes and plans for the future. Legal liability is irrelevant. All that matters is moral responsibility, and for me the only important question is, 'Why was I so stupid?' I have often struggled to find an answer, but I cannot.

And the stress of waiting for trial and the experience of prison have obviously taken their toll, left their mark on me. The memory of both becomes more remote with every passing day, but I still feel violated and defiled by my imprisonment. This sets me apart, and so does my distrust of policemen, lawyers and prison officers. I can respect individuals, but not the system as a totality. I know that the emperor is naked, that most things are a sham, a pious smoke screen billowing around a hard core of cynicism, inefficiency and underfunding.

It is now a year to the day since I was released from prison. I have frequently been asked whether my experiences have changed me, and that is a question I still feel unable to answer. Having benefited from so much friendship, I have learnt to try and be a better friend to others. I am more involved in the affairs of my local community. And although I still have my passion for history, I think I have gone some way towards achieving a better balance between the world of work and striving and the intimate sphere of family, friends and recreation. This makes me less inclined to think in terms of what the cheerleaders of capitalist economics call 'deferred gratification'. Nurture plans and hopes for the future by all means, but make sure that every day contains something that is of value in its own right.

Since my release, I have also devoted a lot of intellectual and emotional energy to this book. Why did I write it? For three reasons. First and above all, I was outraged by the way our motoring laws work and wanted to explain my reasons. I realise that my chances of achieving change are negligible, but I felt that it was my civic duty to make what little contribution I could and I hope that what I have written on this subject will make the reader think.

It was for this same reason that I wrote two articles for the press, and gave a half-hour interview to BBC television, broadcast some months after it was recorded, about my experiences. I also wrote a paper outlining my views on the motoring laws which I was able to submit through my MP to the Home Office and the Attorney-General's Office. I received lengthy and courteous replies which did not really address my arguments and which made it clear – in the nicest possible way – that no account would be taken of them. I had expected nothing else. That was not the point. At least I had tried.

There is a crusading element in what I have written about the law, but I hesitate to express much by way of an opinion about criminals, the prison system or crime prevention. I have no specialist knowledge and I am very aware that my exposure to prison life was brief. Accordingly, I've tried to stick to straight reportage about prison. Just tell it as it is, as I saw it.

But it would be idle to pretend that I have not become strongly committed to the cause of prison reform through my experiences. Overcrowding, twenty-three-hour bang-up and squalor produce degrading and dehumanising conditions. I cannot accept the moral value judgement that degrading conditions are part of the punishment. I see loss of liberty as the punishment and regard it as a stain on our pretensions to being a civilised society that prisoners should be treated like beasts of the field. If the prison population is to remain at its present size or continue to grow, it is morally imperative that more prison officers are recruited so that inmates can spend more time outside their cells and that more prisons are built so that every prisoner can occupy a single cell.

But, of course, I don't believe that our prison population should continue to grow. I cannot believe that acceptance of human waste and broken lives on such a scale is either sensible or moral. In the last year or so, the Home Office has been making spasmodic and incoherent noises suggesting that it can see this too. After the unrelenting illiberalism of criminal policy in the Nineties, the Home Office now seems to be going round and round in circles and occasionally a human face makes a fleeting appearance, like a glimpse of stocking top. Now we hear terms like 'custody minus' and 'custody plus' bandied about, and there is a lot of talk about training and education, better supervision in the community, giving offenders an opportunity to break out of the cycle of crime and imprisonment. Personally, I would add another suggestion to the picture. Drug addiction is behind so much crime that it would make sense to create a parallel network of prisons that are in practice closed drug rehab clinics.

Will anything come of all this? I doubt it. An increasing number of politicians may will the ends, but they do not will the means. The resources required to make custody minus and custody plus work will not be made available, and all we will get are paltry genuflections in their direction. Does that then mean that more money will be spent on creating a civilised prison system? Of course not. Underfunding will remain the dominant factor in crime policy, and things will go on as they are.

My second reason for writing this book was that I thought readers would be interested by my description of trial and prison. I also hoped they would be able to empathise, to understand the trauma of suddenly finding yourself responsible for three deaths and facing criminal charges. Partly, this was because I believed most drivers could see themselves in my shoes. I also expected that many people would relate to my story in another way. Here was 'a middle-class professional man in early middle age' who had never believed it possible that he might risk and experience imprisonment. That changed within seconds, and I thought the story of how some of the foundations of my life gradually crumbled beneath my feet and how I responded to prosecution and imprisonment would speak to others who regard themselves as law-abiding and therefore invulnerable citizens.

Thirdly, I wrote the book in the hope that doing so would enable me to achieve closure. When I started, that went hand in hand with another goal, one that possibly contradicted the first – I wanted the book to be raw and savage and subversive, to express my continuing rage and alienation. One of the titles I originally considered for this book was 'No morality tale'. As a marketing ploy, it would have been a bummer, but what I meant to convey was that I intended to eschew the pious formula of transgression leading to downfall, bitterness and despair followed by ultimate acceptance and spiritual rebirth. This was not to be the story of how

I had become a better and wiser person.

Somewhat to my surprise, as this book has gone through successive drafts, its tone has become gentler. I trust that the process has not gone too far and that the claws of the text, though trimmed, can still be glimpsed. There is an old Swedish proverb that 'when the devil grows old, he enters a monastery'. I would hate anyone to think that of me. This particular devil is still in business, and I hope some whiff of sulphur arises from these pages.

The laws of defamation played a role in this process, naturally, and the book has become more polite – especially about the police, the authorities at Ford and my employers – than I would have liked it to be. But there is more to it than that. The act of writing has helped me to come a long way towards accepting viscerally what I have always understood intellectually – that my travails were trivial and trifling when compared to the destruction of three lives through my agency and that I have been extraordinarily lucky. I could so easily have died or been hideously maimed in the accident; the remainder of my life could have been laid waste by a long and traumatising period of imprisonment. And with that has come acceptance that none of the disasters that befell me and my family really matter very much in the broader scheme of things.

That doesn't make this a morality tale or me a better and wiser man, but it does mean that I can end on a more upbeat note, with some hint of reconciliation. Much of the bitterness, alienation and hatred that weighed on my heart has been purged. And on that foundation, I do believe that I can begin to close the chapter and move on.

27 September 2002

In case of difficulty in purchasing any Short Books
title through normal channels, please contact
BOOKPOST Tel: 01624 836000
Fax: 01624 837033
email: bookshop@enterprise.net
www.bookpost.co.uk
Please quote ref. 'Short Books'